Canadian Tax Paper No. 67   April 1982

The Revenue Budget Process of the Government of Canada: Description, Appraisal, and Proposals

Douglas G. Hartle

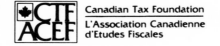

Canadian Tax Foundation
L'Association Canadienne
d'Etudes Fiscales

ISSN 0008-512x
ISBN 0-88808-009-3

Foreword

Of all the matters with which Parliament is concerned, none touches the public to the same extent as the matters now dealt with in the budget. It is the major tool of the government for implementing fiscal, economic, and social policies and often involves decisions of national and international significance.

The procedures by which the federal government reaches expenditure decisions were considered in a study by Douglas G. Hartle, *The Expenditure Budget Process of the Government of Canada,* which was published by the Canadian Tax Foundation four years ago. Curiously, despite its crucial importance, the revenue budget process has been largely unexplored territory. It is paradoxical that a process which is so public in its effect has been so private in its operation. Doubtless one of the factors that has inhibited comprehensive investigation of the procedures of decision making in tax policy is the secrecy that has traditionally shrouded the development of tax measures.

The purpose of this volume is to provide a description and analysis of this vitally important aspect of government activity. The study is based largely on interviews with, and comments by, former government officials and other knowledgeable individuals. The author discusses the process of information collection, compilation, and analysis; examines the roles of organizations and participants both in and out of government who shape tax policy; and identifies the main problems and the process of economic policy making in general and tax policy making in particular. He outlines and critically appraises proposals for reform of the budget process and concludes by offering his own suggestions for improvement.

Douglas G. Hartle is Professor of Economics at the University of Toronto, Associate of the Institute for Policy Analysis, and Research Director and Executive Secretary of the Ontario Economic Council. He served as Research Director of the Royal Commission on Taxation and from 1969 to 1973 was Deputy Secretary of the Treasury Board.

Christine Purden copy edited the manuscript for publication and Marjorie Robinson prepared the index.

As with other Foundation publications, the views expressed in this volume are those of the author and should not be ascribed to the Foundation or its members.

D.J. Sherbaniuk
Director
April 1982

Contents

Foreword. iii
Preface vii
Acknowledgments. xii
Introduction. 1

1   **Sources of Economic Intelligence and Pleading** 6

  The Department of Finance and the Bank of Canada 8
  Provincial Input 10
  The Department of Finance and Other Federal Departments 12
  Taking the General Public Into Account 16
  Other Sources. 20
  Models 20
  Putting the Information Together. 21

2   **Producing a Revenue Budget** 24

  The Budget Stance. 24
  Timing 25
  From the General to the Specific 26
  The Budget Committee of the Department. 26
  The Minister and the Prime Minister 27
  The Cabinet 30
  Parliament 30
  Overview 31

3   **Appraisal and Evaluation.** 34

  Quality of Decision Making. 34
  Budget Complexity 35
  Uncertainty 35
  Tax Expenditures 35
  Integration of Monetary and Fiscal Policy 36
  Dependence on Personalities 36
  Jurisdictional Disputes 37
  Budget Secrecy 39
  Accountability 42
  Summary. 45

4 Proposals for Reform 47

    Pre-budget Reform 48
        Appointed Committees. 49
        Parliamentary Committees 51
    Changes in Budget Content and Presentation 55
    Post-budget Reform. 57

5 Conclusions 61

    Some Alternative Frameworks of Analysis 61
    The Politics of Anticipation. 63
    The Reduced Jurisdiction of the Department of Finance. 66
    Secrecy 68
    Budget Process Reform. 70

Preface

This study has a long (too long!) and convoluted history. It began as a proposal to the Laidlaw Foundation in January 1975—a proposal that was accepted.[1] At that time, I was writing a description and analysis of the expenditure budget system of the Government of Canada for the Canadian Tax Foundation.[2] It seemed appropriate to extend the work to encompass the revenue budget process. Neither had been comprehensively investigated. Yet it would be difficult to argue that the processes themselves did not have a significant impact on the outcomes.

Because there was virtually no descriptive information on the revenue budget process in the public domain, the study of necessity had to be based, at least in the first instance, on interviews. Interviews were arranged with 12 individuals. None of those approached declined. The interviews were carried out by Raisa B. Deber and were taped and transcribed. They began in the summer of 1976, and the final interview took place in January 1978. Professor Deber was selected for the assignment because of her professional qualifications in the use of interview techniques. The interviewees were promised that their identities would not be revealed unless, having seen a draft of the study, they chose to have their names associated with it. This assurance was deemed necessary to obtain frank and full disclosure.

Of the 12 interviewees, only one refused to allow his name to be revealed. The 11 individuals who did choose to be associated with the study are identified in the following list:

The Honourable Walter L. Gordon
Minister of Finance, 1963-1965

The Honourable Mitchell Sharp
Minister of Finance, 1965-1968

The Honourable John N. Turner
Minister of Finance, 1972-1975

---

[1] The grant was to the Institute for Policy Analysis of the University of Toronto, where the research work was carried out.

[2] D. G. Hartle, *The Expenditure Budget Process in the Government of Canada*, Canadian Tax Papers no. 60 (Toronto: Canadian Tax Foundation, 1978).

D1   At what level and how thoroughly? You put great weight on this study.

Robert B. Bryce
Deputy Minister of Finance, 1963-1970

H. Ian MacDonald
Deputy Provincial Treasurer of Ontario, 1967-1974

Albert A. Breton
Professor of Economics, University of Toronto, and adviser to the Privy
Council Office, Ottawa, during much of the period covered by the study

Wayne Cheveldayoff
Formerly Ottawa Bureau, *The Globe and Mail,* and currently Bank of Canada

David K. Foot
Associate Professor of Economics, University of Toronto

Richard G. C. Johnston
Associate Professor of Political Science, University of British Columbia

David M. Nowlan
Professor of Economics, University of Toronto

John A. Sawyer
Professor of Economics, University of Toronto

In the spring of 1979, David A. Good's dissertation entitled "The Politics
of Anticipation" became available.[3] This was an independent study of the
federal revenue budget process, started about a year after the Laidlaw grant
was made but at about the same time as our interviews began. Good's work
was based on many more interviews than is this study—most of them with the
current (at the time) officials of the Department. (D1) His perspective was
different from the perspective taken here, with the result that the two studies
do not end up at precisely the same place. The emphasis and coverage are different. Nevertheless, on those factual matters covered by both sets of interviews, no significant differences were found. The principal differences in interpretation are identified in the text of this study.

Most of the information garnered from our interviews, supplemented
where necessary by Good's dissertation, was embodied in a draft of chapters
1, 2, and 3. This draft was reviewed by a former Deputy Minister of Finance
who had not been interviewed. On the basis of the detailed comments received,
factual errors or ambiguities were corrected and the reviewer's opinion on
matters of interpretation incorporated into the text. The revised draft was
then circulated to all of the original interviewees plus 13 other individuals

---

[3]David A. Good, "The Politics of Anticipation" (Ph.D. dissertation, University of
California, Berkeley, 1979). This dissertation was published in 1980 under the same title
by the School of Public Administration, Carleton University. The references in this study
cite the pagination of the dissertation.

who either had been involved in the federal revenue budgetary process or were particularly familiar with it. All were asked for detailed comments and/or a general statement.

Twelve sets of comments were received—seven from interviewees and five from others. None of the readers submitted a general statement. The names of the seven interviewees who provided comments are Walter Gordon, Mitchell Sharp, John Turner, Robert Bryce, David Foot, John Sawyer, and Richard Johnston. The individuals who were not interviewed but provided comments are the Honourable Donald S. Macdonald, Minister of Finance, 1975-1977; T. K. Shoyama, Deputy Minister of Finance, 1975-1979; a former senior official,[4] Privy Council Office; Patrick Grady, a former senior official, Department of Finance; and J. H. Perry, a former Department of Finance senior official.

Confidentiality was again guaranteed, for the reasons stated earlier; but as the comments were to be published as part of the study, commentators were offered the option of being directly identified with their remarks. Few were willing to have *any* of their comments attributed to them. In the interest of maintaining the confidentiality of the sources generally, while keeping the notation manageable and preserving the information that can be derived from knowing all of the comments attributable to each commentator, it was reluctantly decided that no comments should be attributed to a particular individual unless all could be attributed. This does a disservice to Donald Macdonald and Thomas Shoyama, who were more than happy to be associated with some of their comments. Both Richard Johnston and Patrick Grady asked to be associated with all of their comments. Under the code adopted for this paper (described below), the former is identified as A3; the latter, as O1.

All comments received (other than those dealing with simple factual or grammatical errors) have been reproduced on the left-hand (facing) page and referenced by code letters and numbers to the appropriate paragraph, sentence, or word in the text to which they apply. The temptation to revise the text to permit the deletion of some critical comments has been resisted, for reasons that will be set forth below. The references to the comments are coded as follows:

Former ministers (four)	= M plus numeral
Former deputy ministers (two)	= D plus numeral
Former senior Finance and Privy Council officials (three)	= O plus numeral
Academics (three)	= A plus numeral

I recognize that most readers will find it burdensome at times to have to jump back and forth between the text and the facing comments. The problem is particularly acute when many comments are made about the material on a

---

[4] Name withheld to protect confidentiality.

page, as is often the case. Losing one's place is all too easy. There are, however, so many comments and some of them are so lengthy that inserting them into the text would have posed even greater problems of comprehensibility for the reader. I can only hope that the reader will find some of the comments as fascinating as I did and the payoff worth the extra effort.

Some unique features of the text itself must be drawn to the reader's attention. As explained earlier, and as the footnotes attest, the first three chapters of the text are based on Raisa Deber's interviews for this project and David Good's dissertation. (Chapter 4 is derived primarily from published sources.) *It is important to emphasize that in the preparation of the draft sent to the commentators—that is, with the most minor of exceptions, the text reproduced here—all the significant observations included in the interviews and those found in Good's dissertation were incorporated.* Where I added some of my own comments, I attempted to identify them as such. The same is true of the comments received. Not one of the interviewees complained that something he had said had been omitted from the text. Given the confidential basis of the interviews and the comments, the reader can only be asked to accept this statement on faith; for, unfortunately, I can offer no proof (without breaking my pledge of confidentiality) that this study faithfully sets forth the information and opinions found in the transcripts of the interviews and in the comments received.

In drafting the text, I did not attempt to produce a balanced manuscript that would be acceptable to those who know the most about the revenue budget process. This decision was based on two considerations. First, a draft based on the *selected* observations of interviewees (plus those derived from Good) would have, in some sense, broken faith with them. Second, a cautious and fully balanced draft would not have elicited interesting comments. Here I have a confession to make: the draft was consciously prepared so as to aggravate the most informed commentators to the point where they would react, but not to the point where they would throw it down in disgust and refuse to respond. (Sad to say, it did engender the latter reaction in one instance.) The point is that the comments were envisaged as being an integral part of the study and not as the raw material for a substantive revision or an afterthought. It was never my intention to amend the draft on the basis of the comments in order to produce the "perfect" text. The views of former ministers, deputies, and others about the revenue budget process are interesting in their own right and provide insights into the whole decision-making process of the federal government, of which the revenue budget is but one—albeit an important—example.

As will be discussed briefly in the Introduction and in the text itself, there have been some alterations in the revenue budget process in recent years. In particular, in the 1977-1979 period, there seems to have been greater involvement of the "inner cabinet" in establishing the revenue budget stance and of other departments in devising tax structure modifications. The most dramatic

M1   All to be drafted by the new Liberal government?

D2   This was associated with the Crosbie budget of December 1979.

M1   I have a feeling the Bank of Canada has been a more independent and therefore a more powerful force. But then I think the Bank's policies have been dis-
astrous. See studies by Donner-Peters and Barber-McCallum.

D2   But won't opening up the whole budgetary process as urged in Chapter 4
(and implied by criticism of budgetary secrecy paranoia) lead to even further
erosion and difficulty in maintaining a reasonably co-ordinated view? Doesn't it
often mean simply another forum for the pleading of special-interest groups?
O3   But this can only be done with the active co-operation of all the economic
departments.
M3   Agreed.

developments, however, have occurred within the executive branch with respect to the expenditure budget. These have been reflected in organizational changes: creation of the Office of the Comptroller General, with a massive program evaluation mandate, in 1978; establishment of the Board of Economic Development Ministers (BEDM)[5] in 1978; and introduction of the Clark cabinet committee structure with staffed secretariats for the Economic and Social Policy committees, in 1979. (M1) In substantive terms, the published five-year revenue and expenditure projections, the published estimates of tax expenditures, (D2) and the adoption of an "expenditure envelope" system were most notable.

Some of these changes have or potentially could have profound implications for the role of the Department of Finance. In the summer of 1979, I undertook to revise my expenditure budget book to incorporate these changes. My intention was to combine in one volume the revised expenditure budget material with the revenue budget material included in this study. Although most of the work had been done, this more grandiose project was abandoned. There were two reasons: it was discovered that too many of the vital decisions concerning the "new" system were still pending; and the defeat of the Conservative government in December 1979 raised vital questions about the permanence of the seemingly dramatic changes that had been introduced by that administration. In a year or two, when perhaps the system is once again in a steady state, the more ambitious project will be revived.

In my opinion, the role and authority of the Department of Finance have been substantially eroded over the past decade or so. (The virtual unilateral authority given to the Minister of Finance to allocate funds among the expenditure envelopes could be a reversal of the recent trend.) One can argue that the Department's jurisdiction was too large, its monopoly of some major policy issues too complete, and its pre-emptive powers unsustainable, particularly in an age of prime ministerial pre-eminence, massive government involvement in the economy—both in breadth and in depth—and increasing sophistication of the officers of other departments (of which there are now many) in matters economic. (M1) There is a danger, not so much that the Department as an institution will be emasculated, but that the traditional functions of the Department—particularly in striving (with less and less success in recent years) to integrate overall government economic policies—will not be performed at all. (D2, O3) This could have serious long-run consequences. (M3) It is important that the reader keep this wider perspective in mind when considering the revenue budget process; clearly, it does not take place in a vacuum.

---

[5] The Liberals subsequently renamed this agency the Ministry of State for Economic Development. In January 1982, its role was further widened and the name changed to Ministry of State for Economic and Regional Development.

Acknowledgments

I wish to acknowledge my gratitude to a large number of people. First of all, I must mention the contribution of the interviewer, Raisa Deber, and the 11 interviewees whose names are cited in the Preface. Similar acknowledgment is due to those interviewees who provided detailed comments on the earlier draft and the other five readers named in the Preface.

As well, I wish to acknowledge the contribution that David Good's dissertation has made to this study. As the reader will quickly discover, many of the former actors in the revenue budget process take strong exception to some aspects of Good's interpretation of it. Nevertheless, his work was of great value to me.

For assistance with this study, I would like to mention especially the contribution of Daniel Vincent, Research Assistant extraordinaire. It is doubtful that the project would ever have been brought to fruition without his help. The typing/data-processing skills and efforts of Lorelle Triolo, Judith Kent, Nancy Savoie, and Nancy Cole were prodigious and greatly appreciated.

Last but certainly not least, I wish to express my appreciation to the Laidlaw Foundation. Without the financial support of the Foundation, this study would not have been undertaken.

It is customary for an author to take full responsibility for all errors of omission or commission. While this is sometimes grossly unfair, as a traditionalist I believe I should conclude with the same caveat, and do.

M3   Emphasize.

Introduction

This paper has a three-fold purpose: to describe both the basis on which and the process by which the revenue budget of the Government of Canada was produced until the defeat of the Liberal government in the spring of 1979; and to summarize the principal criticisms of that process and the proposals for change that have been advanced. The utility of obtaining informed views about reform proposals is obvious. Not surprisingly, however, it has been discovered in the preparation of this paper that the same phenomenon has been perceived differently by different participants. In part, this reflects differences in their roles or vantage points. Partly, it reflects the unique circumstances— economic and political—in which each budget was prepared. Personalities changed too, and this was undoubtedly a significant factor. Whatever the reasons, an attempt has been made in writing the description to set forth explicitly these differences of understanding or interpretation with an identification (albeit anonymous) of the source—ministerial, official, or outsider. In some instances, at least, these differences in view provide an insight into the differences in the roles of the players. "What you see depends on where you sit."

This paper seeks to describe the budgetary process from the election of Lester Pearson's Liberal government in 1963 until the transfer of power to the Conservatives in June 1979. As far as is known, the *process* described here was little different from that which existed in the preceding decades.[1] Moreover, although more sophisticated analytic techniques became available in the 1960s and 1970s, as did more data to which they could be applied, the process itself did not undergo radical alteration. What seems to have occurred, primarily as the result of the creation of a formal cabinet committee structure following the election of the Right Honourable Pierre Elliott Trudeau in 1968, was the gradual emergence in the late (M3) 1970s of more cabinet input into the budgetary process. Until then, the content of the revenue budget was determined unilaterally by the Minister of Finance with the concurrence of the Prime Minister on the budget's major thrust and timing. Other ministers were not consulted prior to formulation of the revenue budget and were informed of its content only a few days before it was presented to Parliament by the Minister of Finance in his budget speech.

---

[1] This view may prove incorrect when Robert Bryce publishes the history of the Department of Finance in the earlier period, upon which he is now working.

O1   This seems to imply that other ministers are still excluded. It is not consistent with the statement on the previous page that the creation of the formal
cabinet committee structure following 1968 has led to the gradual emergence in
the late 1970s of more cabinet input into the budgetary process. I would argue
that in recent years cabinet input in the budget process has been substantial.

M4   I've always considered this principle to have been exaggerated beyond common sense. How serious really was Hugh Dalton's indiscretion? Leaks should be
considered on their merits—not absolutely.

A1   Isn't this whole "separation of Finance" not a true delegation, but the result of a tradition evolved in England, of the relationship of the purse to the
Crown?

M2   And in their own interest.

M2   Those who do not share the secret cannot be blamed for the leak.

M1   The concept of budget secrecy is overdone. My experience was that the
Minister of Finance could not count on the support of other ministers because
they were not consulted from the beginning.

Given the enormous impact a budget can have on the fate of a government, not only in terms of the popularity or unpopularity of particular tax measures, but also with respect to the revenues available to finance new vote-catching programs and the perceived effects on such problems as unemployment and inflation, it seems, at first blush, remarkable that prime ministers have accorded such virtually pre-emptive powers to one of their ministers. When one realizes that, at least until recently, the Prime Minister's concurrence has been based on a private, verbal briefing by the Minister of Finance on a subject that has many highly technical aspects, the degree of trust implicit in the delegation of budget authority is little short of astounding. It also says something about the nature of cabinet government that other ministers whose own fortunes could be profoundly affected by a budget apparently have acquiesced in a decision-making process from which they have been effectively excluded—again, until recently.

One obvious reason for the existence of this seemingly anomalous situation has been the long-standing and deeply entrenched budget secrecy imperative. (O1) Parliamentary tradition has dictated that the Minister of Finance resign should *any* of the contents be leaked before the budget is presented by him in the House of Commons. (M4) The tradition is based on the sound proposition that insiders should not have prior access to information that might be used for private gain. (A1) Although all cabinet ministers are under oath not to disclose what transpires in Cabinet or the contents of cabinet documents, one might suppose that denying them access to budget information until the eleventh hour is prudent. (M2) The more who share a secret, the less likely it is to remain secret and the more difficult to identify the culprit and hold him accountable. (M2)   (M1)

One may be permitted to speculate that there have been other and perhaps more significant reasons for the exclusion of other ministers from the budgetary process. Cabinet government involves a complex mixture of the adversarial and collegial approaches to decision making. Ideally, the members of a Cabinet represent in microcosm all of the conflicting interests of the electorate. This representative role of each Minister is partly embodied in the attributes of the individual: sex, age, religion, language, region, and so on. It is also embodied in the Minister's portfolio. The Minister of Agriculture, by the nature of his office, is required to press upon the Cabinet the interests of agriculture; the same is true of the ministers of Labour, Fisheries, Industry, Trade and Commerce, and so on. The decision-making process would collapse if these conflicting interests were not pressed with great vigour. On the other hand, the Minister cannot long remain in office unless these conflicts are resolved—resolved in the sense of mutually accommodated. What must emerge is a series of rolling compromises that, taken as a package, is more attractive to the swing voters in swing ridings upon which electoral success depends than are the alternatives that opposition parties portend. Should a Minister or group of ministers "over-

M2   In my experience, the Prime Minister always supported the Finance Minister in Cabinet when overall economic policy was under discussion.

M4   In my time the Minister of Finance and President of the Treasury Board were a "no team." Literally one [of us] would always stay [in Cabinet committee meetings] to insist that the guidelines were being respected.

O1   Since 1967, the President of Treasury Board shares the role of "no" man with the Minister of Finance. Perhaps this should be brought out [here].

M1   Correct!

M4   And in my observation the Prime Minister did not falter in his support.

M2   The formal fiscal framework introduced in the last decade is a device to remind the Cabinet of the budgetary stance adopted by the Minister of Finance and subject to review as circumstances change. It can be and has been violated, contrary to the rules of the Minister of Finance, but that is not surprising! The Cabinet is prepared to give the Minister of Finance authority with input to taxes but not with input to every expenditure.

M4   Not in 1976-77. Substantially the course that we set was undeflected by the rather general discussion in Cabinet in the weeks before the budget.

O1   It is stated [earlier]. . .that there was "some shift toward the 'full collegiality' model" of cabinet decision making on economic policy. Then. . .it is implied that the "full collegiality" model was actually in effect. This is inconsistent with [the] earlier statement, and probably at odds with the actual situation. The Minister of Finance still has the initiative in fiscal and economic matters and also has a much larger say than the other ministers.

D1   The Department of Finance was a spending department in the 1960s.

D2   The Department of Finance was a spending department in the 1960s (e.g., fiscal transfers, municipal grants, multilateral foreign aid).

achieve" in the pursuit of a few interests, the "successful" ministers will, of course, ultimately defeat themselves with the ministry.

Most ministers hold spending portfolios; they advance the special interests they represent by persuading the Cabinet to increase the expenditures that benefit those interests. It is essential to counterbalance this strong and persistent pressure that would, unless controlled, result in ever-higher taxes and borrowing that would defeat the government. In order to leave the Prime Minister free to shift the balance between spending and restraint, the Minister of Finance must be granted extraordinary powers by the Prime Minister. (M2) If the Prime Minister were to be the perpetual "no" man, his manoeuvring room would be eliminated, and ministers would be inhibited from pressing their special interests. (M4, O1)

The cabinet model just described is collegial only in the sense that other ministers acquiesce in the exercise of pre-emptive powers by the Minister of Finance that are delegated to him by the Prime Minister. (For this model to work, the Prime Minister must *never* falter in his support of the Minister before his other ministers.) (M1, M4) Another model is conceivable. Indeed, in the 1976-1979 period, it seems possible that there was some shift toward the "full collegiality" model. By this term is meant a system in which ministers collectively seek to arrive at some consensus with respect to the appropriate budgetary stance and the Minister of Finance prepares the budget accordingly. (M2, M4) One might wonder, however, if this was not a temporary aberration. Public opinion was so strongly in favour of expenditure restraint that even the most aggressive spending Minister was unlikely to press the case against restraint. But circumstances alter cases. It is by no means obvious that the "full collegiality" model would function in more normal circumstances. (O1)

Another reason the Minister of Finance has traditionally been given massive pre-emptive powers may be the politically unrewarding nature of the task. The portfolio is extraordinarily heavy in terms of workload and extraordinarily light in terms of political rewards. It is well-nigh impossible to be both a popular and a responsible Minister of Finance, at least for a sustained period. Yet the capable performance of the task is of vital importance to the ministry. Only able men can be appointed. Would such men be willing to serve if they were not granted extra powers and could thereby be partially rewarded with the extra prestige that accompanies the office?

As everyone is well aware, the extent of government involvement in the economy increased exponentially throughout the 1960s and the first half of the 1970s. New programs, new departments, and new agencies came into being with amazing rapidity. The Department of Finance, which traditionally had played the role of economic manager for the government as a whole, found itself increasingly extended, particularly with respect to resisting expenditure increases and co-ordinating the activities of other departments with interrelated programs. The responsibilities were reduced in some fields. (D1, D2)

D1   This understates its significance and really occurred earlier when George Davidson was there.

D2   This one sentence should be expanded into a whole set—including appointment of Minister, an elaboration of Secretariat, including the Planning Branch of the Treasury Board Secretariat.

O2   The TBS was removed from the Department and given a separate spot.

D1   And given a separate Minister.

D2   The expansion of the PCO was an important factor as well—necessary as it might have been.

A1   The attempt to set up this independent advisory group was not to advise on taxation, tax structure, revenue, etc., but [to advise] on macro-economic policy, which was deemed inadequate.

D1   What about the Bank?

D2   Fiscal policy, yes, but what about the Bank and monetary and debt management policy?

D1   Department of Regional Economic Expansion (DREE) and Minister of State with co-ordinating responsibilities—Urban Affairs, Science and Technology.

D2   Also the proliferation of government objectives and program agencies; for example, the Canadian International Development Agency (CIDA) with ambivalent mandates, and new enlarged quasi-independent Crown corporations such as [the] Export Development Corporation. What about DREE and [the] succession of ministers of state with co-ordinating roles—Urban Affairs, Ministry of Science and Technology.

D2   Mid-1970s is more like it.

D2   I always tried to listen—but resisted ministerial initiatives raised in Cabinet without prior consultation with [the] Minister of Finance.

D2   Bank and monetary policy.

D2   As far as I can see, it never came to a real test.

O1   . . .In point of fact, while it is true that the government has granted significant tax concessions over the last few years in response to representations from various groups, the increase in the deficit has resulted from a conscious decision by the government to stimulate the economy. This is indicated by the fact that large across-the-board cuts in the personal income tax in 1974 and in the sales tax in 1978 were the biggest components of the discretionary increase in the deficit.

The Treasury Board Secretariat (TBS) was set up as a separate agency in 1967. (D1, D2, O2) The Federal-Provincial Relations Office was established as an adjunct to the Privy Council Office (PCO). (D1, D2) In 1978, the Board of Economic Development Ministers was created to co-ordinate so-called economic programs. Although there were no threats (other than an attempt to set up an independent advisory group reporting to the Prime Minister's Office) (A1) to Finance's exclusive jurisdiction over short-term stabilization policy, (D1, D2) there were some tentative attempts by other departments to break the Department's absolute monopoly of tax *structure* policy. (D1, D2) These attempts were strongly repelled until the end of the 1970s, (D2) by which time the informal proposals of other departments were frequently given sympathetic consideration. (This is not to say that the *technical* opinions of other departments were not sought in earlier years on possible tax measures about which they had special knowledge. Usually, however, Finance asked for opinions on each of a set of alternatives in order to avoid revealing its intent.) (D2)

There is little doubt that the overall jurisdiction and authority of the Department of Finance declined in the late 1960s and in the 1970s. (D2) One reason the revenue budget process has remained so seemingly immutable, particularly with respect to tax structure policy, is the vigour with which Finance, at both the ministerial and the bureaucratic levels, has defended this exclusive jurisdiction. The Department has had a long and honourable history, repeatedly repelling over the decades the endless assault upon the public purse of the barbarous spending ministers. Small wonder that there has been such strong resistance to sharing this responsibility.

Just before the Conservatives' fateful budget of December 11, 1979, a set of tax expenditure estimates was released by Finance. It was decided by the Clark government that cabinet committees would be required to deduct proposed tax expenditures from their expenditure envelopes (that is, the funds allotted to a policy area for allocation among competing programs old and new by cabinet committees). (D2) This suggests that the Department, in recent years, has been under increasing pressure from other departments and cabinet committees, no doubt in response to more stringent expenditure control, to grant tax concessions—tax concessions that, of course, are reflected in the large and persistent deficit. (O1) The adoption of the envelope system of expenditure budgeting (which was associated with the Clark government's strengthened cabinet committee system) and the explicit treatment of tax expenditures occurred after June 1979, the termination date for this study. The reader would be well advised to watch developments in this area under the new Trudeau regime. It would be surprising if the system reverted completely to the pre-Clark situation, particularly because some of the Clark government's innovations were, in fact, being developed within the PCO and Finance before the May 1979 election.

M1   Good.

M4   The Minister of Finance doesn't, in my opinion, gain from secretive pre-paration of the budget. If his advisers are wrong, it's the Minister who is punished, not (until Grant Reuber) those who gave bad advice. I would sooner have a much more candid pre-budget exchange of opinions out in the community.

M1   Good.

M2   I doubt it.

D2   Was Mr. Fleming less cautious?

M4   The reason for not changing more rapidly was the pressure of other busi-ness (the anti-inflation program, the Bank Act White Paper, and federal-provincial fiscal arrangements) and also the fact that there was no preliminary agreement on greater openness in budgeting. When a lawyer and accountant were brought in from outside to deal with the complexities of life insurance taxation, there was a Conservative question of privilege complaining about violation of budget secrecy!

M2   But not, I suggest, because of freedom of information limitations.

M4   An unwise suggestion, like a lot of the other things in the report. (Not one of the major economic factors which have bedevilled the economy—exchange rate and interest rate fluctuations, oil embargos, or oil pricing—could have been anticipated.)

Former Finance Minister Donald Macdonald, in his budget speech of May 25, 1976, called for the abandonment of undue budget secrecy. (M1, M4) The Honourable John Crosbie said the same thing in his December 11, 1979 budget speech. (M1) The Conservatives' Freedom of Information Bill, had it become law, presumably would have had implications for budget secrecy too. (M2) Liberal administrations have been extraordinarily (notoriously?) cautious in this area. (D2) Where more openness in government is concerned, no doubt experience has been a hard teacher and earlier lessons have been well learned. Although one is not sanguine about any dramatic move toward more openness in government generally under the new Liberal administration, (M4) a reduction in undue budget secrecy does not seem improbable. (M2)

The report of the Royal Commission on Financial Management and Accountability (the Lambert Report), issued in the spring of 1979, proposed that the government of the day release a detailed five-year fiscal plan.[2] (M4) As is briefly discussed in the text, the fateful Crosbie budget of December 11, 1979 went some distance in this direction. Will the new administration backtrack? The same report advocated greatly strengthened parliamentary committees; in particular, a "Standing Committee on Government Finance and the Economy" was proposed. This Committee would have reviewed the fiscal plan. The Conservatives tabled a bill that went a considerable distance in this direction. It died on the Order Paper, of course. A number of the procedure proposals (summarized in Chapter 4), which were drawn from a wide variety of sources, emphasized a strengthening of parliamentary committees in the review of proposed or actual tax structure legislation.

---

[2]Canada, Royal Commission on Financial Management and Accountability, *Final Report* (Ottawa: Supply and Services, March 1979), recommendations 5.1-5.6.

D2   Regulation (e.g., controls).

D1   We could also add to this list: increase or decrease taxes because of the ex-isting levels of deficit/surplus and public views about it. (Finance ministers were sometimes old-fashioned and were not following sophisticated policies.)

D1   Incomes policies?

D2   E.g., unemployment insurance, Canada Pension Plan changes.

1

Sources of Economic Intelligence
and Pleading

The revenue budget simultaneously serves five general purposes. These, roughly stated, are to provide the government with an opportunity (or, on occasion, impose an obligation) to:

1) describe and interpret the major economic events of the recent past and the government's view of the economic outlook (frequently with the intent of altering private expectations);

2) congratulate itself for any past improvement in the state of the economy and shift the blame for any past deterioration;

3) announce changes (including no change) in fiscal policy (tax/expenditure/borrowing/lending) (D2) designed to stabilize the economy; (D1)

4) propose changes in the tax/tariff structure designed to

   a) implement social (income/wealth redistribution) policy, (D1, D2)

   b) implement economic (resource allocation) policy,

   c) eliminate "technical" flaws or difficulties with existing tax/tariff structures; and

5) deal with special measures such as incomes policy, federal-provincial fiscal relations, pensions, and special studies.

It cannot be emphasized too strongly that the budget is the result of both an analytic exercise and a political exercise. One can assume that the officials seek to offer the best analytic advice they can muster and that the Minister seeks to bring his best political judgment to bear in the preparation of the budget. Obviously, the ideal budget from the point of view (or views) or officials who are economists is most unlikely to be politically acceptable. Conversely, the most politically expedient budget almost certainly is most unlikely to be without adverse economic consequences—consequences that may be visited on the Minister and the government.

Persuasion, dissembling, logrolling, strategic behaviour, and compromise are necessarily involved in budget speeches for the simple reason that, virtually without exception, policy change will not command universal support. There are almost always some losers; and, hardly surprisingly, this fact has to be hidden, or downplayed or rationalized or offset—actually or perceptually. Indeed,

D1   Some changes are made "after" basic tax. And what about corporate tax?

D2   Also corporate tax for eight provinces.

D1   Do they really? I doubt it.

M4   A perversion of the basic principle. See previous comments above.

D1   When did this last happen in Canada?

O1   Over the last few years, the Minister's responsibilities with regard to budget secrecy have been interpreted less strictly than in the past. The federally funded retail sales tax cut in Mr. Chrétien's April 1978 budget was reported in the *Toronto Star* prior to the budget and Mr. Chrétien was not forced to resign. It was widely recognized that, if the federal government were going to have joint fiscal action with the provinces, it would be impossible to avoid the risk of a leak and, if a leak were to occur, it would not necessarily be the responsibility of the federal Minister of Finance. Also, there was an allegation of a leak after the December 11, 1979 budget based on a CTV news report by Craig Oliver prior to the budget. The resolution of this affair was that Mr. Crosbie directly and categorically denied that there was any leak for which he assumed responsibility. This satisfied the Speaker, who would not take action which would amount to a contradiction of the word of the Minister of Finance unless there were a proposal by the House directly to contradict the Minister's word by accusing him, or someone else, specifically of taking responsibility, or failing in the responsibility to safeguard budgetary secrecy. On the basis of these two incidents, I would agree that there is a significant amount of judgment involved as to what constitutes a leak and that the tradition of budgetary secrecy is being interpreted somewhat more liberally than in the past so as not to stand in the way of effective policy making.

D2   A major problem is that this sound and appropriate tradition has been escalated in Canada by partisan and adversarial politics, but even a leak without these potential consequences is also seized upon for political attack—take the John Reid case, regarding changes in federal sales tax on motor boat engines about 1975 or so.

some voters may be antagonized by the non-announcement of an anticipated policy that would have made them winners or reduced their losses.

The economic analyses and the political analyses that are embodied in the budget depend, of course, on a continual flow of economic and political intelligence. It is vitally important to realize that the budget represents a snapshot, so to speak, of a never-ending process of information collection, compilation, and analysis. Political and economic strategies are constantly being devised, implemented, and revised in response to changing economic and political circumstances. Finance ministers and their officials have to cope with policy making in a most uncertain world. Because it is an uncertain world, where expectations drastically affect economic behaviour, not only do the budget makers have to take into account, as best they may, changes in the volatile expectations of investors and others; they also have to recognize that the contents of the budget itself, and indeed its tone as distinct from content, can radically and quickly alter those expectations. The Department's need for "soft" as well as "hard" economic intelligence is therefore great.

Because most tax/tariff measures are announced in the budget speech, and because these changes can profoundly influence the distribution of income and wealth of groups of individuals and businesses, the Department has always been the target of special-interest groups pleading for favourable changes. Provincial governments are vitally interested in the federal government's fiscal policy and tax/tariff changes: the former can significantly affect their revenues and expenditures; and the latter can affect their revenues, in particular because the federal personal income tax (PIT) tax base is also the PIT base for the provinces (with the exception of Quebec). (D1, D2) Other federal departments and agencies also have more than a passing interest in the decisions incorporated into the budget. Changes in the level of economic activity can change dramatically the demand for some government services (for example, manpower training). (D1) Certainly, tax and tariff changes can complement or offset the expenditure programs and regulations administered by other agencies.

From this general perspective, I shall now examine in more detail some of the particular continuing interfaces that have existed between the Department and "the rest of the world." In considering these relationships, the reader should constantly bear in mind the enormous importance that has had to be attached to budget secrecy by officials and ministers alike. Although one can argue that secrecy surrounding some (most) aspects of the budget is unnecessary, and indeed perverse, the fact that the resignation of the Minister was and still is mandatory if it should be discovered that *any* budget information has been leaked has ensured that secrecy is not only a rule but almost a fetish. (M4, D1, O1) As was stated earlier, the severe consequences that flow from a breach of budget secrecy are based upon parliamentary tradition—a tradition that reflects the impropriety of providing prior information to a few "insiders" from which they can profit, often at the expense of the many. (D2)

D1   The Bank too has a tradition and practice of keeping its mouth shut.

M2   The Governor of the Bank is in a unique position among the advisers of the Minister of Finance since he comments publicly, from time to time, through his annual report and otherwise on the state of the economy and the appropriateness of fiscal and monetary policy.

D1   The Governor has a legal obligation to consult.

D1   The Minister can and does argue in private with the Governor.

A2   This agreement began in 1961, with Rasminsky's appointment. It did not exist when Coyne was Governor.

D1   It is much more important that he sits in the Executive Committee of the Board every week, which he does in the same capacity.

D2   Understated. The degree of informal consultation from the professional working level right up to the very top was very extensive.

D1   The borrowing operations involve frequent meetings and occasions for some general policy discussion.

D2   Only appropriate details.

M4   His participation must have been with departmental officials. If the Governor knew he did not discuss the proposal with me.

D1   During the war—J.R.B. sometimes took part in the detailed discussions.

The Department of Finance and the Bank of Canada

The relationship between the Department of Finance and the Governor of the Bank of Canada is unique in that the Bank is essentially the only entity with which Finance has fully and freely exchanged information. (D1) Although the Minister of Finance has been ultimately responsible for the policies of the Bank, there also has been a recognition that the Bank should remain independent of narrow political pressures. (M2) The balance between autonomy and political accountability has been maintained by allowing the Governor of the Bank a free hand in formulating day-to-day monetary policy. (D1) If the Minister of Finance were to disagree with the direction of the Bank's overall policy, he would be required to issue a public statement ordering the Governor to alter it. (D1) The Governor would then have to either follow the directive of the Minister or resign. (A2)

This peculiar relationship has been one of the reasons the two institutions have remained so closely in touch. Each seeks to avoid, if at all possible, confrontation; consequently, neither has wished to surprise the other by unilaterally taking action that has not been thoroughly discussed beforehand. Though the Deputy Minister of Finance has sat as an ex officio, nonvoting member of the Bank's Board of Directors, (D1) most of the contact has been informal. The Minister has met in private with the Governor about once a week, and his Deputy or Assistant Deputy Minister usually has had lunch with officials from the Bank about twice a week. (D2) Debt policy (D1) and exchange operations both require the closest collaboration between the Department and the Bank at the working level. The Minister is responsible for both, but both are inextricably related to monetary policy; furthermore, the Bank acts as the government's agent in carrying them out. In addition, officials from the Department's Economic Analysis and Taxation divisions have often consulted staff of the Bank's Research Department.[1]

Close communication has been essential, not just to guard against unintended major policy differences, but to facilitate the co-ordination of fiscal and monetary policy. The Governor has been one of the few people outside the Department privy to the details (D2) of an upcoming budget. (M4) During and in the years following World War II, he has sat in on discussions of budgetary policy and offered advice as to the appropriate fiscal policy, bearing in mind the implications for monetary policy. (D1) Currently, however, as one senior official remarked, "This does not occur inevitably, consistently and regularly." Though Finance officials may not always follow the Governor's recommendations, any fiscal decisions they do make must take into account his policies.

---

[1] Robert J. Bertrand, Alice Desjardins, and René Hurtubise, *Legislation, Administration and Interpretation Processes in Federal Taxation*, Study for the Royal Commission on Taxation #22 (Ottawa: Queen's Printer, 1967), 31.

D2   Pre-1974-75, [a] "credit conditions" approach was used. This was before the focus on money supply targets—but [the] same factors [were] involved.

A1   You could be sure of inequity only if these had not been inequitably acquired.

D1   This is putting it in very specific terms for the unsophisticated.

D1   What about the long period when "credit conditions" and not targeted growth in M1 provided the criteria for policy?

D2   A completely inaccurate accusation in my observation!

D2   Not as far as I was concerned!

D2   Wrong. In my experience, they never intruded, but I invited their views.

D2   Right—in former periods, I understand, the Bank participated in discussion of structural and program issues.

M2   What does this mean? What kind of formal mechanism? The Governor cannot and should not control fiscal policy. The Minister can control monetary policy by issuing directions. There is a very formal mechanism now in existence, and that is the Minister of Finance supported by his colleagues.

D2   Completely unfounded claptrap. We always emphasized to ministers the uncertainty of cash flows in the Exchange Account so as not to mislead or disguise.

D1   And the Bank's balance sheet and government's cash balance are published every week.

M1   This doesn't mean much.

D1   I don't think this is correct. In my experience, they have nearly all gone to Cabinet (but not Treasury Bill sales)—but there is little that ministers are usually able or willing to say. An order in council was required for new borrowing.

The "bottom line" of the fiscal framework statement published with the budget speech is the net cash requirements of the coming fiscal year. Should cash be required, the Minister can order the Bank, as the government's fiscal agent, to carry out the requisite debt issue(s). The crucial question—the question on which the Bank's independence has been tested—is the extent to which the Bank will accommodate the increased debt by increasing the money supply. Too much accommodation would, over time, result in inflationary increases in the money supply that would mean, in essence, that the government was being financed by an inequitable hidden tax on fixed income assets and workers with lagging wages. (D2, A1) Although there were undoubtedly other factors involved, it was to minimize this danger that the Bank was given a degree of autonomy. (D1)

There have, however, been some problems with the relationship. The Bank has been accused of a persistent bias toward price stability and thereby of giving too little weight to problems of unemployment.[2] (D1, D2) This may have been the source of some friction between the Department and the Bank. (D2) The Bank of Canada's strong economic analysis program, combined with direct access to the Minister, undoubtedly has given it an influential advisory role.[3] Some observers have noted an attempt on the Bank's part, in the latter part of this decade, to increase its say in the making of overall economic policy. (D2) A long-time senior official much closer to the situation has remarked that except for debt and exchange management, where collaboration is inescapable, the Bank is far more remote from policy making than it was 15 years ago. (D2)

The informal nature of the relationship has also been criticized. One official observed that the closeness of the relationship has been dependent, not surprisingly, upon the personalities involved. He believed that the quality of the relationship between the two institutions had varied drastically with changes in the top men in each organization. Another observer criticized the fact that there has been no formal mechanism for the integration of fiscal and monetary policy. (M2) Because the integration has been done in the heads of a few top officials, he claimed, it has been possible for them to disguise (D2) how the government was actually financing some of its activities. It is by no means clear how one should interpret such a statement. Because the Bank engages in foreign exchange transactions virtually every day, it is buying or selling Canadian dollars. When Canadian dollars are purchased, those dollars can be used to finance government expenditures; however, the status of the exchange fund account is published each month, so that any "disguising" is of an extraordinarily short-term nature! (D1) In recent years at least, all major debt issues have received prior cabinet approval. (M1) This probably was not the case in the past. (D1)

---

[2] Richard W. Phidd and G. Bruce Doern, *The Politics and Management of Canadian Economic Policy* (Toronto: Macmillan, 1978), 248.

[3] Ibid., 175.

D2   Also to improve economic intelligence and forecasting.

M2   They try!

D2   When? My impression is that we were active on both fronts continuously from the late 1960s up to the present—including debt management and exchange rate policy.

A2   The neoclassicists are winning out over the Keynesians!

D2   What does this mean?

D2   And frequently quarterly.

The Bank of Canada has played a major role in a great many of the Department's actions. It has been consulted frequently by the Department for a number of reasons: to avoid potentially embarrassing policy conflicts; to integrate fiscal and monetary policy; and to gain the Governor's advice on the Department's proposed deficit. (D2) Though there has been no open conflict between the two organizations since the Coyne affair in 1961,[4] one could speculate that with a declining role played by fiscal policy as a stabilization instrument, the influence—indeed, power—of the Bank has risen commensurately at the expense of the Department of Finance per se and the Minister. On the other hand, and probably more important, the Bank too has adopted a policy of increasing the money supply within stated bounds and has disavowed "fine tuning." The fact of the matter is that neither fiscal policy nor monetary policy is now used as actively as it once was. (M2, D2, A2)

Provincial Input

The relationship between the federal and provincial levels of government has been both extensive and pervasive with respect to financial matters—probably more so than in other fields. The Department of Finance has "consulted" its provincial counterparts more freely than other outside interests; however, the adversarial nature of the relationship on most issues has undoubtedly meant that consultation has been, in fact, a one-way street (D2) or a negotiating session. A former provincial official identified three main arenas in which interaction has taken place. The first has been the renewal or renegotiation of the Tax Collection Agreement and the Fiscal Arrangements Act and Equalization. Second, there have been meetings to develop solutions to specific policy problems, such as a "stop-gap anti-unemployment measure" and tax reform. Finally, the most important forum for discussing financial relations between the federal government and the provinces has been the federal-provincial Continuing Committee on Fiscal and Economic Matters (CCFEM) set up in 1955.

The CCFEM has been composed of senior civil servants from the Department of Finance and the provincial treasuries and has been chaired by the federal Deputy Minister of Finance.[5] It usually has met at least twice a year. (D2) The Committee's primary responsibility has been to exchange and discuss information on the economic and fiscal issues to be dealt with in a meeting of the Committee of Ministers of Finance and Provincial Treasurers that normally has followed. A number of subcommittees of the CCFEM have been

---

[4]For a discussion of the Coyne incident, see Peter Newman, *Renegade in Power* (Toronto: McClelland and Stewart, 1963), 295-321.

[5]For a more detailed description of the history, composition, and responsibility of this Committee, see A. R. Kear, "Cooperative Federalism: A Study of the Federal-Provincial Continuing Committee on Fiscal and Economic Matters," in J. Peter Meekison, ed., *Canadian Federalism: Myth or Reality?* (Toronto: Methuen, 1968), 305-17, at 305.

O1   The meetings of the Continuing Committee at which the proposal to index the personal income tax to inflation [was discussed] took place after the announcement of indexing in the February 1973 budget.

D2   During the period of implementing tax reform.

D2   Its general policy intent—i.e., fiscal stance—but not specific measures.

M4   Early in the calendar year.

M2   As to proposed tax changes or any other legislation that may be amended in his budget speech.

D2   Particularly in recent years.

O1   In recent years, first ministers' conferences have come to be less focussed on "specific policy issues." The first ministers' conferences on the economy in February and December of 1979 were fairly general in orientation.

formed to deal with topics such as economic analysis, investment policies, and intergovernmental taxation, or other more specific issues that may arise from time to time.[6] Though the Committee's main function has been to resolve administrative problems (and it has been quite successful in this role),[7] it also has discussed some policy matters. For instance, the proposal to index personal income tax to inflation was debated quite hotly at these meetings. Ultimately, though, the federal Department of Finance chose to override the objections of the provinces and implement indexation. (O1)

The CCFEM has established the agenda for meetings of the Committee of Ministers of Finance and Provincial Treasurers. Previously, this ministerial Committee met quarterly, (D2) but the recent trend has been toward semi-annual conferences. The federal Minister of Finance has chaired the Committee. He has used it primarily to inform the provinces of Ottawa's view of the economic outlook and Ottawa's intended policies, (D2) and to give his advice on how the provinces should react. The provinces have similarly provided information on their economic analyses, forecasts, and policies, and expressed their views (that is, criticisms or agreement) concerning the federal government's actions. Usually one of these meetings has been a pre-budget conference, and the federal Minister of Finance has been able to give some general indication of the direction his budget will take. (M4) Despite the fact that these meetings have been confidential, in providing such information the Minister has been bound by the rules of budget secrecy. (M2)

Some discussion on economic matters has taken place at the annual Plenary Conference of Premiers and Prime Ministers (D2) (this conference has tended to deal with specific policy issues) and at other ad hoc top-level conferences, such as the informal conference concerning the implementation of wage and price controls in October 1975.[8] (O1) It seems, though, that the lower-level meetings—in particular, the closed meetings of the CCFEM—have been the most valuable in promoting better co-operation and co-ordination.

Because the Deputy Minister normally has accompanied his Finance Minister to the ministerial meetings, in addition to attending the CCFEM meetings, he has met formally with his provincial counterparts at least four times a year. As Edgar Gallant has pointed out, however, informal contacts such as telephone calls, letters, or visits play a significant role in federal-provincial economic relations as well.[9] The amount of this type of interchange has varied, of course, with the personalities involved.

---

[6] Information obtained in interviews and from an Ontario government official.

[7] Supra footnote 5, at 316.

[8] R. D. Olling, "Canadian Conference Activity 1975: Alberta Participation," in J. Peter Meekison, ed., *Canadian Federalism: Myth or Reality?* 3rd ed. (Toronto: Methuen, 1977), 229-38, at 230.

[9] Edgar Gallant, "The Machinery of Federal-Provincial Relations I," in Meekison, ed., supra footnote 5, 287-98, at 290.

D2   Not in my view, except insofar as provinces discounted or disclaimed any responsibility for stabilization policy.

O1   Focus of the regular meetings of deputies of BEDM was primarily on microeconomic issues and policies. Thus, it [the Secretariat] did not really displace the DM10.

O3   Not really, because the economic deputy ministers were primarily focussed on macro issues. BEDM committee focusses on micro case work.

D1   When I was Deputy Minister, I was quite prepared to listen to the views of other departments on what we should do, just as I was prepared to comment on what they should do.

D2   Not in my time from 1968 onward, and only in regard to specific tax changes at budget time, if at all.

M2   Have provincial ministers of finance informed the federal Minister of the tax changes they will propose in their budgets?

D2   This is a curious interpretation. If the quote is from a provincial Minister, it neglects the fact that often there were *10* provincial ministers who wanted to talk, especially when they had criticisms or complaints to offer. In recent years, the federal Department took the lead in organizing written material.

In 1935, Mackenzie King stated that

> A Dominion-Provincial Conference is neither a cabinet nor a Parliament. It is an institution which enables the Government of Canada and the governments of the Provinces of Canada to confer together and to exchange information. . . .[10]

This has remained an important purpose for federal-provincial conferences dealing primarily with economic stabilization policy, although, speaking more generally, this purpose has gradually become less important as more and more issues have become negotiable. (D2) One former Minister noted, "I did more listening than talking at these meetings."[11] None of the parties involved at these meetings expected to be able to influence directly the economic policies of the other participants; however, by providing information about their own policies, they could be certain that these factors would be taken into account when the other parties were making decisions.

The Department of Finance and Other Federal Departments

There has been a curious ambivalence about the relationships between the Department of Finance and other federal departments. Although most departments have had a real and inherent interest in the activities of Finance (some, of course, more than others), there also seems to have been a tendency to shy away from direct attempts to advise or influence the Department on major fiscal and tax policy matters. At least, this was the case until the continuing committee of "economic deputies" became active in the mid-1970s.[12] This Committee was, in effect, displaced when the Secretariat to BEDM was created — the Secretariat that served Mr. Clark's Cabinet Committee on Economic Development. (O1, O3) The new structure not only allows, but actually requires the heads of the relevant departments to advise and seek to influence structural economic policy. One might speculate that the reason departments were previously reluctant to try to influence Finance was that such attempts were frequently rebuffed, and not always gently. (D1) In earlier days, Finance officials were inclined to treat such overtures in the same way as a judge might treat a phone call from an interested party in a case before him. (D2)

---

[10] R. M. Burns, "The Machinery of Federal-Provincial Relations II," in Meekison, ed., supra footnote 5, 298-304, at 302.

[11] This comment may substantiate the provinces' complaint that they provided much more information than did the federal Department of Finance at their meetings. (M2, D2)

[12] This Committee was established by the Secretary to the Cabinet, Michael Pitfield, who acted as chairman at the outset. Gradually, however, Thomas Shoyama, then Deputy Minister of Finance, assumed the chairmanship.

D1   Energy, in recent years.

D2   But frequently only at the last moment before discussion by cabinet committee.

D2   Not so—we were frequently confronted at the last moment with final revisions.

D2   Major input at these earlier stages was of the essence.

M4   The fiscal package relating to the energy proposals contained in the May 1974 budget was prepared after close and careful exchanges between Finance and Energy, Mines and Resources. That relationship was enhanced by the relations between [Messrs.] Austin/Reisman, Shoyama/Reisman.

O1   Copies of the memoranda to Cabinet are sent routinely to all ministers and departments. Thus, Finance is not unique in having access to cabinet memoranda. Where Finance differs from other departments is that Finance has the staff and expertise to take a critical and independent view of other departments' proposals. Because of this, departments will provide draft cabinet papers to Finance to get a reaction. If this reaction is not favourable, the departments will often consider modifying or even dropping proposals. This process of feedback helps to avoid unnecessary conflict in Cabinet.

D2   I wonder.

The line departments, however, have always provided Finance with considerable specific information arising from their operations or collected by them to assist them in meeting their own responsibilities. Manpower, housing, and construction data are examples. (D1) Copies of the memoranda to Cabinet prepared by all departments have been sent routinely to Finance before being considered by ministers collectively. (D2) This has provided some opportunity for the Finance Minister to be briefed in advance of the meeting and for him or his Deputy to state the Finance view before a decision is reached. It should be emphasized, however, that these memoranda rarely have contained new information. (D2) Finance officers usually have been monitoring (D2) departmental policy proposals throughout their development and have often tried, with greater or lesser success, to influence them at earlier stages. (M4, O1)

The most important means of information exchange and co-ordination of economic management has been interdepartmental committees. Although there has been a great deal of ebb and flow in the significance of particular committees of officials, as suggested above, the most powerful committee probably was DM5, (D2) the committee of deputy ministers formed from DM10 to monitor post-control policy and boards,[13] such as the Regional Development Incentives Board (RDIB).[14] Colin Campbell and George Szablowski in their study of central government agencies, *The Super-bureaucrats,* claimed that committees "were the principal means of communication and deliberation" among departments.[15] They were able to distinguish almost a hundred of these organizations. The committees serve as sources of information, opportunities to influence policy, and ways of facilitating the policy-making process, and they provide a means of gauging policy performance. It is therefore not surprising that Finance officials attended more committee meetings than did any other officials or that they were involved in the widest range of subject areas. It is also notable that Finance officials, more than any other officials, felt that they were able to influence directly policy decisions at these meetings. The committees usually have been composed of 10 to 15 civil servants of similar rank. They have met regularly and have had relatively informal mandates. Interdepartmental committees of ministers have been appointed by the Prime Minister (or the Cabinet), who has also appointed the chairman. Interdepartmental committees of officials normally are appointed by the Secretary to the Cabinet, probably after consulting the Prime Minister in the case of committees that are thought to be of major significance.[16]

Information also has been gained more informally through interchanges primarily among officials from the planning branches or the economics divi-

---

[13] Colin Campbell and George Szablowski, *The Super-Bureaucrats: Structure and Behavior in Central Agencies* (Toronto: Macmillan, 1979), 151.

[14] Supra footnote 2, at 295.

[15] Supra footnote 13, at 148.

[16] Ibid., 147-49, 166, 179-80.

D1   Not often, in my experience.

D2   Not so, as far as I was concerned. I didn't try to flimflam like this at all.

M2   Most departments have specific responsibilities and objectives. Agriculture
has to advance the interest of farmers, Industry of manufacturers, and so forth.
Finance has a general responsibility for overall economic policy which takes into
account these specific interests. It is natural, therefore, that Finance officials do
more listening than talking at interdepartmental meetings. Somebody has to put
it all together for assimilation by the Minister of Finance. The alternative is a
committee of officials that has to revise the spending departments' interests and
to come up with a consensus. Small wonder they are content to let Finance take
the responsibility and the blame.

D2   Only with regard to tax matters, and even here I disagree with any suggestion of closed minds or ears.

O2   An example is the lack of interest by other departments on the subject of
tax expenditures.

sions of the various departments. Such informal methods, however, have become less prevalent, giving way to a more rigid, formal structure.[17] When the Finance Department has required information on specific issues or proposals that has not been forthcoming in the normal course of events at official meetings, it has employed other tactics. If the issues have been highly political and potentially embarrassing, the Minister or his Deputy has informally asked the advice of a very few influential ministers.[18] If Finance has sought another department's view of a specific proposal, it has, on occasion, (D1) obliquely consulted it, perhaps by hiding the specific proposal among four or five others.[19] (D2) Information thus has been gained without indicating the Department's real intentions.

The deployment of this tactic emphasizes the nature of the traditional relationship that has prevailed between the Department of Finance and the other departments. Although the Department has been able to influence greatly the policies of the other departments and gain much information from them, the reverse has not been true, generally speaking. Line departments have neither had much influence on nor gained much information from the Department of Finance. (M2, D2)

David Good claims the departments were not *too* dissatisfied with this situation. In particular, he reports that outside officials seemed willing to accept their lack of influence on Finance, particularly on taxation matters, (O2) and he cites a few possible reasons. First, the benefits to the other department gained from such items as tax expenditures were generally perceived as slight. Second, and following from this, because most ministers and probably outside officials were not sufficiently well informed to criticize Finance's policies, they felt the benefits were not worth the additional efforts and embarrassment that might result by pursuing the tax expenditure issue. The seeming lack of interest of the other departments in tax expenditures also may have been the result of their unwillingness, in part, to enter into a comparison of the effectiveness of direct expenditures relative to tax expenditures. A simple reason may, however, be the best. The decision-making machinery did not provide other departments with an occasion to discuss tax expenditures, at least until after the event. This weakness, if you like, was attributable to the budget secrecy requirement. Because most policy changes are irreversible in the near term, discussion of them after the event would be treated as idle.[20]

---

[17] Ibid., 151, and information obtained in interviews.

[18] David A. Good, "The Politics of Anticipation" (Ph.D. dissertation, University of California, Berkeley, 1979), 222.

[19] Ibid., 228, and information obtained in interviews.

[20] Ibid., 168-71.

D1   Fiscal policy was an important influence.

D2   We had fiscal policy objectives that were not inconsistent with selective tax reductions. We "acquiesced in face of pressure" only for films and multiple unit residential buildings, and to some extent on energy conservation and research and development.

O1   Pressure from other departments and from other groups for tax expenditures was a consideration in the decision to release the discussion paper on the tax expenditure account along with the December 11, 1979 budget. However, it was only one of a number of considerations. Ministers had earlier expressed an interest in tax expenditures. Thus, work on tax expenditures had been going on in the Department for a number of years. This work paralleled that going on in other countries, and it took its inspiration from a common intellectual pool. That the tax expenditure account was published in December 1979 reflected more the timing of the completion of the departmental work and less a strategem on the Department's part to defuse mounting pressure for tax expenditures. In addition, the integration of tax expenditures into the new expenditure management system did not necessarily result [from] pressure from Finance. Rather it could be viewed as a natural development of the logic of the new system.

D1   In the 1930s, 1940s, and 1950s, the Minister and chief officials took a considerable part in budget discussions.

D1   Also the Minister of National Revenue.

O1   The Department of External Affairs does not arrange all tax conferences. Even in the case of the Canada-U.S. tax treaty negotiations, External's involvement has not been large.

D1   Also Agriculture and Fisheries.

D2   We were in particularly close consultation with Energy, Mines and Resources on energy pricing and taxation, with Manpower and Immigration on unemployment insurance and employment programs, with DREE, with Transport, with the Ministry of State for Science and Technology, Agriculture, etc.

Good's perception, based on interviews in 1975, was that the interest in tax expenditures appeared to be increasing. There is no doubt that this departmental pressure increased extremely rapidly in the 1977-1979 period, the period of expenditure restraint. The acquiescence of the Department in the face of this pressure resulted, (D1) of course, in the erosion of revenues with a resulting increase in the deficit. (D2) It was to counter this pressure that Finance prepared estimates of tax expenditures (released just before the December 1979 budget) and pressed for a policy that all future increases in tax expenditures be deducted from one of the expenditure envelopes assigned to each of the several policy fields. This certainly would tend to reduce the internal demand for additional tax expenditures. (O1) Indeed, it might reverse the pressure. Spending ministers may press for the reduction or elimination of particular tax expenditures with a commensurate increase in the size of the relevant expenditure envelopes. The Minister of Finance would then have to bear the hostility, and the spending minister(s) would bask in the glory of expanded expenditure programs.

A few departments have been much more aware of and concerned about the actions of the Department of Finance than have others. The reason is that the decisions of Finance have directly affected their operations. The Department of National Revenue, for example, has been responsible for administering the taxation policies of Finance. Finance therefore has consulted Revenue to determine whether there are any anomalies or loopholes in the current Income Tax Act that should be changed and to ensure that any proposed changes are administratively feasible.[21] (D1) The Department of Justice (D1) has been responsible for the actual drafting of tax legislation, and there usually has been an official from that Department working with Finance to confirm that any proposed changes are constitutionally and legally sound and to ensure that in the drafting the actual motion reflects the intention of the Department of Finance.[22] The Department of External Affairs has arranged all international tax and trade conferences and has had an obvious interest in all international economic matters. (O1) Apart from the U.S.-Canada agreements, the bilateral tax treaty discussions have involved External in only a limited way. The negotiating has been done by Finance officials. Similarly, Industry, Trade and Commerce (D1) is vitally concerned with tariff questions because changes can create opportunities and/or problems for that Department's clientele. (D2)

Conflict has at times arisen over the Department's jurisdiction because of these closer relationships. Robert Frost believed that good fences made good neighbours. Unfortunately, departmental jurisdiction can seldom be defined so precisely, nor can roles be so independent. Jurisdictional competition is as inherent in political/bureaucratic (nonmarket) decision making as is price

---

[21] Ibid., 180, and information obtained in interviews.

[22] Supra footnote 1, at 32-33.

M4   A Finance–Industry, Trade and Commerce–External Affairs rivalry over the multilateral trade negotiations was resolved at the cabinet level by making Allan MacEachen, then President of the Privy Council, the lead Minister.

O2   This would be true of my days in Finance–1936-1952.

M4   As House Leader, I had to prepare the legislative program for Parliament. Finance would come in at the last minute with its own list of requirements and demand–and often get–priority.

D1   I doubt [that] most readers will understand the nature of "operations." The Department wanted to keep itself free from administrative burdens to be able to concentrate on policy.

D1   This was not the case in regard to tax reform.
M3   I initiated formal consultation with the caucus and with financial critics of opposition parties. MPs had scope but often were not asked.

competition in conventional markets. There has been, not surprisingly, a traditional jealousy among Finance, External Affairs, and Industry, Trade and Commerce (and sometimes Agriculture) as to which should have the ultimate say on tariff matters. (M4) The Department of National Revenue, because of *its* particular duties, has had—again, for obvious reasons—a strong interest in advocating both increased tax structure simplicity and a greater *appearance* of equity in the tax system as a prerequisite to the continuation of the self-assessment system. Its advice to Finance, according to David Good's interviews, has sometimes strayed from narrow technical matters to more policy-oriented issues.[23] (O2) The weight accorded to Revenue's views on the latter is an open question.

Statements made by two of our interviewees support the idea that attempts from any quarter to enter the traditional territory of Finance have been met, at least until recently, by the stiffest possible resistance. The Department, through involvement on interdepartmental committees and other, more subtle techniques, has been able to ensure (again, until relatively recently) that it has received the information it requires from other departments for its decision making. But by maintaining close control over the information the Department itself releases, and by carefully guarding against any and all perceived intrusions into its pre-eminent role as manager of the economy, Finance has remained one of the most powerful and independent federal departments—still again, at least until recently. (M4) A former official, however, commented,

> The fact is that Finance has been giving up jurisdictions for years. In some cases the Department actually sought to give it up and has argued the case for giving it up. This is true of all the operational [D1] roles it ever had.

Taking the General Public Into Account

Though David Good claims that Finance has tended to listen to rather than consult outside parties, such as individual taxpayers, MPs,[24] national associations, and lobbies, the Department has not worked in ignorance of the views of these people.[25] In fact, knowledge of the feelings of the general public has been essential in enabling Finance officials to gain a "feel" for the political climate, to allow them to determine what sort of stance to take, to determine what policies would or would not be acceptable. This listening to outsiders

---

[23] Supra footnote 18, at 181-85.

[24] MPs, of course, may be considered as a group separate from the general public. Traditionally, however, they have had relatively little interest in financial affairs, and their influence with the Department has been only marginally greater than that of the public. (D1, M3)

[25] Supra footnote 18, at 165ff.

D2 I don't agree fully with this description. Whenever I received representa-tions, I would try to indicate the nature of a countervailing argument, or at least ask questions about it. In 1971, I shocked the Independent Petroleum Associa-tion by asking if the country really needed to subsidize the oil industry as we were then doing. I "argued" frequently with the small business lobby, the Cana-dian Manufacturers Association, the mining associations, but not in [such] a way as to express a personal view on special tax points.

O2 A key point.

M4 Not totally satisfactory as a justification. Instead of being mute, an official might try the countervailing arguments upon an interviewee without in any sense advocating his own opinions.

O1 Any taxpayer cannot usually obtain a personal interview with the Minister, as suggested here. The Minister is obviously a very busy man and cannot meet with everyone who wants to see him. As a rule, he would meet with a taxpayer only if it [were] necessary to resolve an important matter requiring ministerial attention.

O3 Really?

O2 This correspondence is a remarkably sensitive and ready indication of the public feeling on actual tax issues and was very influential.

has also contributed greatly to their own technical knowledge. Most of this input has come from representations to the Department made throughout the year but particularly between July and February, with a noticeable intensification three or four months before budget day.[26]

The Department has encouraged these representations; but usually, it has not provided the public with the views of officials on the issues being discussed. Instead, the officials have acted as passive observers, listening attentively to complaints without reacting to them. (D2) Although this stance is undoubtedly frustrating to the petitioners, in my opinion it would be improper for the officials to behave otherwise. Decisions are made by ministers on the *advice* of officials. What an official personally thinks about an issue, what he advises his Minister to do about it, and what the Minister decides to do can be, and often are, three quite different things. Where the advice of officials is usually given great weight by the Minister, because of the highly technical nature of the subject matter, for an official to reveal to a particular petitioner what he intended to advise would be unethical. Either everyone outside the Department should know, or no one should know. (O2) Moreover, if officials stated their personal views to outsiders, the appropriate advisory-responsibility relationship between officials and the Minister would be seriously damaged. Either the Minister would be compromised, or he would be forced to discredit the officials publicly. (M4)

Even though any taxpayer can usually obtain a personal interview with the Minister, (O1, O3) complaints from individuals usually have come in the form of letters to the Minister of Finance. The Department has received about 8,000 letters annually, mostly from individual citizens.[27] (O2) Officials have stressed that every single letter has received careful attention and a thorough reply ("even the stupidest things," according to a former official). The Department of Finance has been very concerned that the individual should see that his or her views are seriously considered.

Letters of this sort have been helpful in gauging the current political climate, a matter of particular concern to the Minister of Finance, of course. In addition to these inputs, each Minister normally has had his own favourite group of advisers. Good describes one Minister who simply asked those he met on airplanes for their views.[28] Another former Minister consulted five or six leading economists, as well as the general public, and kept his own "running book of suggestions" that had accumulated throughout the year. One can presume that although an individual supplication has rarely resulted in any action, combined these inputs have generated an overall impression of the electorate's

---

[26] Supra footnote 1, at 33.

[27] Supra footnote 18, at 195-97.

[28] Ibid., 255-56.

O2   Agreed.

D2   We would always be asked, as well, to study briefs submitted to the Cabinet directly (e.g., from the Canadian Labour Congress) and offer briefing comment on economic questions.

expectations—an impression that has been vital in the production of a document as politically sensitive as the budget.

Probably briefs presented by groups or associations have been of greatest direct influence. Our interviews tended to confirm Good's conclusion that the most effective lobbies have been groups that are relatively small and readily distinguishable.[29] Policies that affect them can be easily isolated and identified. These groups know their own interest and can lobby effectively because they are less inhibited by the "free rider" financing problem that bedevils larger groups with more amorphous interests. (This problem is discussed further in Chapter 5.)   (O2)

The annual submissions of the Joint Committee of the Canadian Bar Association and the Canadian Institute of Chartered Accountants have been quite different in character and purpose. These briefs have been concerned primarily with technical problems in the existing tax system—anomalies, complexities, and loopholes. Occasionally, some policy changes have also been recommended. The Department of Finance has been dependent to a not insignificant extent on tax professionals for such information, and officials have attended—usually as observers, but not infrequently as participants—tax conferences such as the annual conference held by the Canadian Tax Foundation (CTF) in the late fall.[30] In addition to tax professionals, briefs from other national associations such as the Canadian Chamber of Commerce, the Canadian Manufacturers Association, and the Canadian Police Association, as well as religious and cultural groups, have been sources of information too, although some of the presentations have taken on a ritualistic quality.   (D2)

The usual procedure that has been followed in dealing with an organization that has a specific problem or complaint—for instance, an industry concerned about a particular tariff—can be briefly described. The group first gets in touch with an official in the Department. Normally, the official then invites the group to draw up and present a brief. If the issue is a purely technical one, the brief might be presented to the Department's officials only. If, however, the issue has policy implications, as is often the case, the brief is presented at a meeting with the Minister of Finance, usually but not invariably accompanied by one or two of his senior officials. The officials listen to the brief and sometimes ask that a few questions be clarified; typically, they do *not* debate the merits of the issue.[31] A former senior official commented on this observation,

---

[29] Ibid., 189-92.

[30] Ibid., 194, 209-10.

[31] Supra footnote 1, at 33-38; Marshall A. Cohen, "Formulation, Enactment and Administration of Tax Changes," in *Report of Proceedings of the Twenty-fourth Tax Conference*, November 27, 28, 29, 1972 (Toronto: Canadian Tax Foundation, 1973), 4-22, at 6; and information obtained in interviews.

D2   I agree fully.

O1   The comments of the former senior official are accurate. Many of the meetings between officials and groups concerned with tax matters do get into substantive discussions of the pros and cons of specific measures.

M3   The declining competence of Finance staff. There has been a dreadful erosion of talent.

The difference between debate and questioning is subtle. Are you (sic)[32] suggesting that the process is to some extent the poorer if a debate doesn't take place? I do not recognize the typical representation in your descriptions. I think there is more give and take with officials than you allow. (D2, O1)

A list of *all* the suggestions is compiled in a volume that has been called at various times a budget book, a black book, or a red book. All these suggestions have been reviewed, with greater or lesser degrees of intensity, by officials for possible inclusion in the budget. (Sometimes, if the problem has required an immediate solution, a ways and means motion has been tabled almost at once.) Of course, not all of the recommendations have been accepted, but none has been completely ignored either.

Most members of the Department stated in their interviews that the public had some influence on tax policy decisions, although it is impossible to gauge how much. Major outcries about specific policies have been known to result in policy changes in the past. In addition, although the Department normally has not consulted outsiders on policy matters, there have been a few situations where it was willing to do so. David Good lists some examples. Generally speaking, consultation took place only when the acceptability of a proposed change was uncertain and the potential for embarrassment was low. If the proposal was found to be unacceptable, the Department was able to retrace its steps without loss of face.[33]

On the whole, however, the pattern of the Department's relationship with outside interests has been that of a passive observer. The Department has encouraged presentations from the public to gain information, not to provide a forum for debate on the pros and cons of alternative "solutions" to the issue at hand. Several reasons have been advanced for this reticence. Some observers have claimed that officials from the Department have not had the resources to deal competently with each issue that is presented. Perhaps they have felt, on occasion, at a disadvantage relative to a private professional who has had access to more data and has been able to devote more time to the problem.[34] (M3) Former officials have claimed that the strict rule of budget secrecy has been the basic reason for their reticence. They have felt that by actively seeking information on particular issues or even by commenting on presentations, they might have been "tipping their hand" and implying what the views of the Department were.[35] Whatever the reason, the technique of acting solely as an information-gatherer has put the Department of Finance in a fairly

---

[32]The commentator used the word "you," presumably meaning the author, but in fact the views expressed were those of an interviewee.

[33]Supra footnote 18, at 219.

[34]Ibid., 190, 194; and supra footnote 1, at 40.

[35]Supra footnote 1, at 40, and information obtained in interviews.

D2   The Department has to brief the Minister to defend his decisions. Usually in Committee of the Whole, the tax officials sit with the Minister on the floor to help provide information, clarification, and explanation.

D2   Much of this whole document deals with the tax methods in the budget. The most significant data source is National Revenue—as published statistics and special runs that can be provided without indicating data on any individual tax-payer.

O1   Other agencies supply data to Finance on a regular basis. The Department of National Revenue should be mentioned for the tax data it supplies.

D1   International Monetary Fund consultations have really been much more serious and useful, and the reports (but they are not published) are distributed to all member countries.

M3   As chairman of the Internal Committee (Executive Chief).

M3   He brought William Hood in as the chairman's adviser.

powerful position. It has had no obligation to deal with any particular suggestion it has received, and has simply been able to pick and choose from its "list" without being under any compulsion to justify the rejection of specific proposals. (D2) There have, of course, been exceptions, where a tax structure issue advocated by an opposition party met with widespread media/voter approval (for example, mortgage interest deductibility).

Other Sources

First and foremost in the list of other suppliers of "hard" data to the Department has been Statistics Canada. This autonomous agency of the federal government produces statistical series, including the principal measures of the state of the economy that the Department is responsible for managing.[36] The data flowing from Statistics Canada are used not only to assess the economic health of the nation, but also to diagnose the symptoms and analyse the potential efficiency of alternative remedies. Finance is only one of a multitude of Statistics Canada clients and, in principle, has no special status; all the data available to Finance are also available to other users. About the only special concession made to Finance by Statistics Canada has been that it has regularly supplied the former (and some other government agencies) with some data a few days in advance of their general release. This has permitted ministers to respond immediately to questions in an informed manner. Even this advantage has been criticized by opposition members. Like other users, Finance has constantly pressed Statistics Canada for more data, and for more reliable and timely data. But Statistics Canada officials have been extremely sensitive to criticism. (D2)

In addition to Statistics Canada, Finance has obtained data and information on a regular basis from the Bank of Canada, Canada Mortgage and Housing Corporation, the Foreign Investment Review Agency, the National Energy Board, and other federal agencies.[37] (O1) International economic organizations also have provided economic intelligence. (D1) The Organization for Economic Cooperation and Development, for example, has provided an extensive appraisal of the state of the Canadian economy and federal stabilization policy. John Turner noted particularly the value he gained from his work on a subcommittee (M3) of the International Monetary Fund. (M3)

Models

Econometric models are another aid to the forecasting and analysis so essential to the decision-making process. The Department of Finance has had access to a number of different models. In 1954, a econometric model was developed

---

[36] Ibid., 32.

[37] Ibid., 110-11.

A1   The main difference, as far as I know, between the RDX models and others rests on the emphasis given in the former to the supply side.

M2   While the annual reports of the Economic Council are usually concerned with the intermediate or longer-term outlook, that body has from time to time influenced current economic policy of the federal government, most notably when from time to time it [has] formulated targets for the level of unemployment. I am inclined to think, for example, that the acceptance by the Council in its first report of a target of 3 per cent unemployment had a significant—and in retrospect an unfortunate—influence upon fiscal and monetary policy in the middle 1960s by calling for increasingly expansionary policies.

D2   And the published Annual Economic Review or the federal-provincial "Brown" and "Green" Books, and the attempt to put together prospective financing requirements on a yearly outlook basis.

in the Department of Trade and Commerce under C. D. Howe and was later "moved" to Finance. It is now passé. Models developed outside the Department are valuable sources of information. The Economic Council of Canada has supplied results from the CANDIDE model and Statistics Canada's SCQEM model has been used. Models that are oriented more to monetary policy— RDX1 and RDX2—have come from the Bank of Canada.[38] (A1) Academic institutes such as the Institute for Policy Analysis of the University of Toronto— which formerly supplied the TRACE model—and the Conference Board of Canada have supplied forecasts and analyses. As well, private research firms such as Data Resources Incorporated (DRI) have provided results from a wide variety of models, and the Department has been able to use DRI models to derive its own forecasts from its own assumptions. The influence of these models has varied. (M2) One official noted that if forecasts emanating from the several models converged (that is, showed similar findings), they had a great deal of persuasive power.

Putting the Information Together

It is beyond the scope of this paper to discuss in detail how the staff of the Department has handled this endless flow of hard and soft information, and derived from it a picture of the past performance of the economy and the most probable future picture in the absence of further policy changes. Nor is it possible to describe here how the Department has analysed the effectiveness of alternative policies retrospectively or prospectively. What is important for the layman to grasp is the continuous nature of the task. Perceptions of the nature of the problem(s) facing the economy (hence the government, hence the Department) have been constantly changing with the degree of consensus among officials about the "Department's view" ebbing and flowing as additional information of all kinds from all sources has come available. Diagnosis, prescription, and decision making have proceeded endlessly and iteratively. Developing documents such as the fiscal outlook[39] and the budget speech (D2) has constituted, in many ways, taking snapshots of an ongoing, ever-changing set of official-ministerial perceptions of the Canadian (and world) economic reality and of their judgments about public perceptions of the same phenomena.

Despite the growing importance of models and formalized government structures, inevitably the final decision is judgmental. A former Minister stated,

> Anybody who is responsible should have as good a set of forecasts as possible and then if they are not satisfactory he should. . .proceed to see how they should be altered. But it's these modifications that tend to be compromises.

---

[38]Supra footnote 2, at 216.

[39]An annual statement to Cabinet on the state of the economy, prepared by the Department of Finance and customarily presented in December.

O1   The experience of recent years would not seem to offer much basis for generalizations about "pre- and post-election" budgets. The post-election budget of November 1974 was one of the most expansionary, containing large tax cuts. On the other hand, the pre-election budgets of May 1974 and December 1979, which brought down minority governments, were restrictive.

D2   Would there have been less criticism if there had been an overestimate?

O2   Usually this resulted from some marginal factors such as the level of corporate profits, personal income, or sales—also, the degree of inflation.

D2   This discussion is just nonsense.

M3   This was not inadvertent, but reflected a decision to roll back on unworkable sections of "tax reform." It was a deliberate decision.

D1   Not really surprising, given the complex nature of the Tax Reform Bill.

O1   The Department's record within the area of tax policy has not been poor. The fact that following tax reform the government had to introduce a large number of amendments to the Income Tax Act is not an indicator of poor tax policy. Rather, it is indicative of the inherent complexity of tax legislation and the necessity of continually amending it to keep it working as intended. The number of amendments to the Income Tax Act could also be seen as a measure of the Department's responsiveness to emerging tax policy issues. Some of the amendments were due to the new provisions rising from new policies. Others were to refine concepts. As well, a number of the amendments were to respond to developments that did not exist and could not have been anticipated at the time a measure was originally introduced. If there had been no amendments and the number of loopholes had been allowed to increase, it would not have been good tax policy.

D2   I would argue [that] the large number of changes shows an openness and flexibility on the part of the Department.

With the rarest of exceptions, policy making, whether or not embodied in budgets, has involved painful compromises. And what has constituted the "best" compromise has been the judgment, for most major decisions, of the Deputy Minister and the Minister of Finance. The quality of the judgment has hinged on the ability of these men to combine technical data and analyses with political savvy. Because of this, still other factors have come into play. The parliamentary timetable has had a significant effect on budgets. Post-election and pre-election budgets have differed vastly in "tone." (O1) As well, the nature of the personalities involved has been very important. Some major policies—such as medicare, the indexing of personal income tax, and the social development tax—were due mainly to the timely (or untimely) presence of one or two men.

The question inevitably arises as to the quality of these decisions in the past. In the realm of economic analysis and forecasting, the Department has been severely criticized. By 1976, the forecast revenues from the Department of Finance had been underestimated in 18 of the 19 previous years. (D2, O2) Some officials blamed unanticipated foreign events and the impact of new programs for the inaccuracies. David Good claimed that they simply reflected the inherent conservatism of the Department.[40] More critically, another observer claimed that it was only one more way in which Finance was able to enhance its power within the government. (D2)

In the area of tax policy also, the Department's record has been rather poor. The Tax Reform Bill of 1971 was followed by 175 amendments in each of the next two years, 146 in 1974, 75 in 1976, and 95 in 1977.[41] (M3, D1, O1) The necessity for these adjustments has led some observers to suggest that the Department change its method of receiving advice and discuss its intentions more freely,[42] an issue to be pursued at some length later. (D2)

Canada has been burdened for several years with significant levels of unemployment and rising prices. Output has grown slowly, and government deficits have increased rapidly. The Canadian dollar has fallen. And the immediate prospects are far from bright. Could these difficulties have been avoided? Did the Department of Finance do as well as circumstances permitted, or has there been economic policy failure? Judged in the light of the performance of other industrial countries, the Canadian record is by no means depressing. But

---

[40] Supra footnote 18, at 48n.

[41] Tax Legislative Process Committee, "The Tax Legislative Process" (March-April 1978), 26 *Canadian Tax Journal* 157-81, at 172.

[42] Ibid., 158-59; and Thomas d'Aquino, G. Bruce Doern, and Cassandra Blair, *Parliamentary Government in Canada: A Critical Assessment and Suggestions for Change*, a study for the Business Council on National Issues (Ottawa: Intercounsel Limited, 1979), 75.

M2   This final paragraph illustrates a point that troubles me about Chapter 1. While the budget is an attempt to bring together all aspects of the economic situation and to lay down the general lines of policy for the future, and the Minister of Finance between budgets has a general responsibility to affect the fiscal framework, he is not the "economic czar." A misjudgment of the market for nickel or aluminum, an inappropriate marketing policy by the Canadian Wheat Board, an increase in the price of imported petroleum, or a series of strikes could be much more important in the economic performance of Canada than anything done in a budget. The comment made earlier about the limitations of fiscal and monetary policy deserves expansion. Moreover, in retrospect, it is evident that the decision to cushion Canadian consumers against rising prices for imported petroleum was probably the most crucial recent decision of the Government of Canada. That was a decision of the government as a whole. The Minister of Finance was not the author; and like the rest of us, he could not have foreseen the full consequences.

had Canada unique advantages (for example, as a net energy exporter) that were not exploited? Or was our economic performance admirable given Canada's unique disadvantages (such as the unprecedented rate of growth of the labour supply)? These must remain unanswered questions for us.   (M2)

M2   And in recent years, the constant checking of expenditures against the fiscal framework has transmitted this stance to at least some members of the Cabinet.

O1   It would certainly be impossible to produce a budget in a few days, even if pressed. As is noted later in the study, it usually takes six weeks to prepare a budget. This period could perhaps be compressed to a month, but not to much less.

2

Producing a Revenue Budget

Little has been written about budget formulation processes as distinct from the content of federal revenue budgets. The stringent secrecy that has prevailed with respect to content before delivery of the budget speech by the Minister in the House has created an aura of mystery about the process itself. Until recent years, officials were reluctant to discuss the process, thus adding to the mystique. Finally, the process no doubt has differed from budget to budget, because of either circumstances or personalities, and this has made generalization difficult. Fortunately, the paucity of information about the process has been largely overcome by David Good, who interviewed a large number of Finance officials and former ministers. The following description draws heavily on his work. It is, however, supplemented by information gathered from the confidential interviews carried out for this study.

The budgetary process is described here, following Good, as a set of discrete steps. But it should be recognized that, in reality, these stages have been amorphous and certainly less rigid than one might infer from the description. The somewhat formalized process described is simply an attempt to impose order on an informal, continuing process/event that has differed to some degree each time it has taken place.

The Budget Stance

Good describes the first step in producing a budget as setting the "budget stance." The implication is that between budgets the Department has had no stance. As has been emphasized before, this is misleading. In a sense, within the Department there has been, at any point in time, a view: (M2) a view that encompasses the nature of the problem, the cause of the problem, and the general kind of policy best able to deal with it. If pressed, Finance could have produced a budget in a few days. (O1) As one might expect, however, the degree of consensus among senior officials and the extent of agreement between the Deputy Minister and the Minister have not been constant.

In the past, the Deputy Minister usually has been able to persuade the Minister and his officials as to the most prudent course in the circumstances; he has aimed to reconcile the political necessities of the Minister with the technical necessities of the officials. What seems clear is that the budget stance, embodying all of the general dimensions just mentioned, has always been ap-

M2   The officials who advised me also gave their personal assessments of the political considerations.

M4   Agreed.

M2   Every year, and the best time to do so is in the spring after the expenditure estimates have been presented to Parliament.

D2   How do you describe November 1974?

proved by the Minister—no doubt with varying degrees of apprehension. Both the officials and ministers interviewed recognized a sharp and valid distinction between their roles. The officials felt that they were responsible for presenting the technical and professional assessment, but recognized that the Minister's politically oriented judgment both should and did have the ultimate authority. (M2) The ministers too felt that their role was different. One described himself as "the behavioural scientist," and another claimed that he offered a sort of tempering influence on the Department's rather impersonal, technical view. Each Minister had his own personal source of information in addition to his Department. One even went so far as to ask other parties to write budgets for him, so that he could better evaluate that produced by his Department. Despite these external sources of information, however, as Good found, ministers normally relied on the advice tendered by their Department.[1] Ministers rarely demanded any major changes in the Department's proposed policies, probably because of a mutual accommodation to the perceived exigencies of the other participant(s). (M4)

Timing

The timing of the budget has been, generally speaking, determined by three factors:

1) The parliamentary timetable: it is expected that there will be a budget speech each spring. (M2)

2) The electoral timetable: something must be given away just before elections, and campaign promises must be more or less kept in budgets shortly following elections.

3) Extraordinary unanticipated problems that require the government to appear to be doing something in response. (D2)

The decision on the budget date usually has followed a discussion between the Minister of Finance and his Deputy. Between them, they have decided upon a deadline date to work toward. The Minister has then discussed the date with the Prime Minister to ensure that it fits in with other government plans. When the date has been confirmed, he has informed his Deputy and work has immediately begun on writing the budget. The time lapse from the initial decision to the budget speech varies from budget to budget, but typically it has not exceeded six weeks.

Once the decision has been made to produce a budget, the normally reticent Department has become almost completely silent. Given the traditional rule

---

[1] David A. Good, "The Politics of Anticipation" (Ph.D. dissertation, University of California, Berkeley, 1979), 256.

D2   Is it paranoia to take steps to be adequately responsible?

D2   Economic analysis.

O1   Budget secrecy is no longer maintained by ensuring that no person works on more than one area of tax policy. There are significant numbers of people in the Department who are familiar with the budget in its entirety. Budget secrecy is maintained by the integrity and professional responsibility of Finance Department officials.

D2   But only after discussion with the Minister on the "stance" and substantive content.

O1   Attendance of Budget Committee meetings varies from one budget to the next and is at the discretion of the Deputy Minister and assistant deputies (particularly those in the key branches involved in budget preparation—the Fiscal Policy and Economic Analysis Branch and the Tax Policy Branch). The Budget Committee is not rigid and formal, but flexible.

of budget secrecy, the violation of which would usually lead to the Finance Minister's resignation, the men involved have been extremely careful, to the point of paranoia, (D2) not to divulge *any* information. Though submissions from the public have increased at budget time, the Department has refused to comment on them; and about two weeks before the budget has been brought down, all outside contact has been cut off.

From the General to the Specific

With the setting of the budget date, it has been necessary to convert the rather vaguely defined stance into precise proposals. For example, the stance may have suggested that, on balance, the budget should be restrictive, but that investment should be stimulated in certain industries and middle income families should not be hit too hard. (D2) At this point, the Assistant Deputy Minister for Tax Policy has become a central figure. He has been responsible for translating, with the help of his own officials, the qualitative budget objectives into more tangible tax change provisions. This has involved innovation, adaptation, and drawing from the lists of possible tax changes—some originating externally and others internally—that the Department has been considering more or less actively. In the past, secrecy has been maintained in his Branch by ensuring that no individual works on more than one area of tax policy. (O1) Technical changes designed to correct anomalies within the system also have been considered. A brief summary of the consequences, both real and apparent, of each possible change has been written and the suggested changes compiled in the budget book as options. This set of options then has been sent to the Budget Committee for consideration.[2]

The Budget Committee of the Department

The Budget Committee has been the main decision-making body in the budgetary process, where "decision" means decision to recommend to the Minister. The Committee has decided which of the options presented will be recommended and the members of the Committee have written the actual budget speech. (D2) David Good claims that the Deputy Minister, the Associate Deputy Minister, all the assistant deputies, as well as at least two directors, have been members of the Committee.[3] (O1) A former top official, though, claimed that he included only those officials he felt were necessary for the specific budget, and often some of his assistant deputies were not involved.

Two features should be noted about the progress of the budget through this Committee. The first is the setting of the budget "tone." Will the budget

---

[2] Ibid., 262-73.

[3] Ibid., 279.

D2   Heavily influenced by the Minister.

D2   Nonsense. My committees frequently had sharp differences of opinion, and I encouraged formal argument and discussion.

D2   Previously discussed and agreed with the Minister.

M3   I recast the draft to reflect the tone I wanted and to make it less bureaucratic sounding. I invariably wrote the introduction and conclusions.

D2   Particularly from the comprehensive view made possible by the draft.

D2   Reconsidered.

D2   Throughout the 1970s, we almost invariably went through at least six or seven drafts, revising both content and presentation.

M2   This is a comparatively recent practice. When I was Minister of Finance, I did not clear the wording of the speech with the Prime Minister. I did, however, discuss the general approach and the specifics of major tax changes.

M3   Not necessarily minor—hinges on the particular Minister. Moreover, I got involved at the earliest stages so the officials knew where I stood.

O1   It is misleading to suggest that the Minister's changes in the budget are "invariably minor." The Minister is involved in the budget process at all stages; and in a parliamentary system such as [ours], his input is obviously key.

be a "we must be steadfast" budget, or will it be a "hallelujah" budget? (D2) Are there any specific areas that the Department wants emphasized more than others? Although the tone has not been unrelated to the budget stance, it has differed in that it has been concerned with the emotional–persuasive quality to be reflected in the speech itself. Vague though it may have been, it has not been unimportant. Good claims that the tone, having been set, has often been the ultimate factor in choosing which specific tax changes are to be made.[4]

Another feature of the Budget Committee that deserves comment is the way in which decisions have been made. Consensus has been striven for and conflict carefully avoided. (D2) Compromises rather than votes or authority have been employed. Good distinguishes a few rules that have been used to facilitate decision making—for example: "the greater the uncertainty, the smaller the tax change acceptable"; "the greater the tax change, the greater the effort to produce a 'balanced' or fair budget." This concern for a balance, giving the appearance that all sectors of society will benefit (or suffer) equally, has been important for all budgets. Obviously, the Budget Committee has worked hard to produce a speech that will provoke a minimum of hostility.[5]

The Minister and the Prime Minister

When the Committee has completed a draft of the budget speech that includes, of course, the specific tax proposals it is recommending, (D2) the draft has been sent to the Minister of Finance for approval. At this stage, as well, the Minister sometimes has had a significant input. (M3, D2) Inevitably, he has rejected (D2) some items and suggested a few others.[6] (D2) As a former Deputy stated, "It [the budget] also reflects the personality of the Finance Minister; it has some of his personal touch in it."[7] The revised draft incorporating the Minister's changes (almost invariably minor) has then been presented to the Prime Minister. (M2, M3, O1)

To reiterate for emphasis: the business of "producing" a budget has been under way long before the decision actually has been made to present a budget speech. In fact, it has been never-ending. As well, the men producing a budget have formed a very small, closely knit community. Informal discussions among all levels from Assistant Deputy Minister to the Minister have been continual. For instance, although the onus for first establishing the stance of the budget has been borne by the Deputy Minister and his assistant deputies,

---

[4] Ibid., 274-78.

[5] Ibid., 279-88.

[6] Ibid., 290.

[7] Ibid., 275.

D2   As I recall, more often than not, the Minister and myself, and on occasion the Governor of the Bank, met with the Prime Minister and his chief officials, to indicate our general views and the options under study—with the Minister usually making the presentation. On a couple of occasions, two or three of the most senior ministers also attended.

M4   Not my experience: several weeks before, general outlines were discussed with the Prime Minister and Clerk of the Privy Council; then, closer to the event, these would be made more specific. Turner started and I continued to give outlines to [the] Priorities and Planning Committee of Cabinet.

M4   I agree.

they have not produced this stance without influence from their Minister; conversely, the Minister has rarely been surprised by the recommendations of his Department. In the same way, the distinction between the stage where the Budget Committee has drafted the budget and the stage at which the Minister has approved it has not been as clearly defined as our description suggests. Dialogue between the Minister and his officials has taken place almost daily. Thus, although the preparation of the budget has followed the general path described above, it should not be inferred that sharp distinctions have existed. The relationships among the principal actors have not been clear cut and rigid.

In some respects, the relationship between the Prime Minister and his Minister of Finance has been similar to that between the Minister and his Deputy: both exhibit a great deal of mutual influence and accommodation. Consequently, it is difficult to specify precisely how much influence the Prime Minister has had on a budget. Once again, there has usually been regular consultation between the two men, ranging from the diagnosis of major economic problems to the decision to produce a budget on a particular date. As has been previously mentioned, about a week before the budget, the Finance Minister has presented his draft speech to the Prime Minister. (D2, M4) Obviously, at this point, very little of significance could be altered without postponing the speech. And postponements have not occurred. If the Prime Minister were to have had any influence, then, it must have been exercised at the earlier stages of the process. The interviewees agreed that the Prime Minister's principal role has been to legitimize the Department's decisions, but there was no consensus as to whether or not he has played a positive role in the decision-making process. One official, according to Good, stated that the Prime Minister's concern was on the "most macro-level."[8] If this is true, his influence most likely has been felt when the stance is being taken. Conceivably, he has been asked informally if he agrees with a general stance. The same official went on to say, "But I've never seen him deny a Finance Minister." A former Minister stated that there had been no instance when the Prime Minister exercised his prerogative and demanded fundamental changes. The impression that most gave was that while they recognized the Prime Minister's right to demand change in a budget, the Department would have been both surprised and annoyed if he had actually done so. (M4)

In summary, the situation that has prevailed, at least until the May 1979 election, and has prevailed for decades (perhaps since Confederation) is captured by the following statement of a former senior official:

I think I could say with confidence. . .that the budgets that were produced during the period I was Deputy Minister of Finance reflected the work of the Minister of Finance and his Department virtually exclusively.

---

[8] Ibid., 299.

M3   Agreed, but post-1975?

O2   In the sense of frequently being a headache—I can recall some pretty exhausting sessions lasting after midnight and for weeks at a time.

D1   It is not sure that budget was the cause, other than just the occasion. See your later comment.

M3   At the pre-budget conference with the Prime Minister, he confined his comments to general stance. He had no interest in tax structure matters.

M3   When Jack Austin, the Prime Minister's principal secretary at the time, attempted to create a semi-formal and permanent advisory group for outside, I was the Minister. I gave [the] Prime Minister the choice between the group and my resignation.

M4   See previous comment about Turner and after. My experience is that the time frame was longer.

Obviously, they took into account views of other departments, and views that they obtained here thither and there, but we're the people who did it, put it together and decided what to do, and that's what was adopted by the Government. (M3)

This is heady stuff, (O2) particularly when it is recognized that only two governments in Canadian history have fallen as a direct consequence of a budget (D1) (May 1974 and December 1979) and that the tax measures proposed in the ways and means motions tabled at the same time are rarely substantially altered as a result of debate in the House (the Gordon budget of 1963 being a notable exception).

That this situation has prevailed is hardly surprising, given the nature of the relationship between the Finance Minister and the Prime Minister, and the near-impossibility of any Prime Minister having enough technical knowledge to grasp the details of the budget. The relationship between the Prime Minister and the Minister of Finance, like that among the members of the Budget Committee, has been one of consensus. All those interviewed stressed that neither man would have allowed himself to be caught in a position from which he could not back down gracefully. The fact is that if a minister has a major disagreement with the Prime Minister, he usually has to resign or to be replaced. No wonder there has been caution on both sides. One official pointed out that it was incorrect to speak of either of them winning or losing arguments, claiming that they were more likely to defer the issues on which they were in disagreement until one or the other had seemed to modify his position. The reasons for the difficulties in specifying the Prime Minister's influence are clear. It is certain that the Finance Minister has been aware of the Prime Minister's view, and vice versa. But it is impossible to determine how much the views of a Minister have been modified to reflect those of the Prime Minister, or to ascertain how much a Prime Minister has accommodated the views of ministers with whom he has disagreed.

The Prime Minister has had neither the time nor the expertise, at least until the latter years of Mr. Trudeau, to criticize Finance policy effectively. No doubt this explains the fact that the Prime Minister has confined his attention to the broad aim and general tone of the budget. (M3) This situation undoubtedly has been changing. As officials have pointed out, in their experience Mr. Trudeau was better informed than his predecessors about specific tax policies. The increasing size and expertise of the PCO staff[9] and Mr. Trudeau's use of independent economic advisers undoubtedly enabled him to ask more searching questions in meetings of the Priorities and Planning Committee. (M3) Whether this kind of probing influenced Finance in preparing its budget is unclear, but it would be surprising if it did not.

---

[9]Ian Stewart, an Assistant Secretary to the Cabinet and economic adviser to the Prime Minister in the 1976-1980 period, was particularly knowledgeable and influential. (M4)

D1   There is one clear case in the "Thirties" re-tax treatment of Mines.

M2   Rather three presentations to the Cabinet: the first, a general survey of the economic situation and outlook and the fiscal outlook; second, a description of the general direction I intended to take; and finally, a day or two before the budget presentation, the tax changes I would propose.

M4   Agreed.

O1   The Minister would as a rule go back to Cabinet in the event of a major change in the economic or fiscal outlook between the Cabinet's last briefing and a budget. The second official quoted was correct.

D2   That is certainly my recollection also.

M4   Especially Priorities and Planning Committee.

D2   Or that the growth of the deficit was a matter for concern.

D2   Declined, not disappeared.

M4   In 1975-1977, the politics of the situation undoubtedly favoured me. Having lost one Finance Minister, the government could not afford to lose a second. Disagreement there might be; but in the end, they made way.

M3   It also emasculated the Department, because the cabinet structure is based on the adversarial as well as the collegial principle.

D1   It's a difficult process for even an honest man.

D2   This was the situation during my period. In fact, we took fiscal policy papers to Cabinet more frequently than once each year, especially if there seemed to be a change.

The Cabinet

There seems little doubt about the extent of Cabinet's influence on the content of the budget: it has virtually none. (D1) This was the situation at least until the last few years of the previous Trudeau administration. The Cabinet has been informed about the general direction of the budget about a week before budget day and has been told the details a day or two before it is brought down. (M2, M4) It has not been asked for its approval in either case. The Cabinet has had an opportunity to infer the intentions of the Department of Finance through the fiscal outlook briefings and the fiscal framework statements.[10] However, even when the economic situation changed in the period between the fiscal outlook briefing in December and the budget preparation in the spring, one former official of the Department stated that Finance did not feel that it was incumbent upon it to return to the Cabinet for confirmation of the new diagnosis or prescription; rather, the Department simply proceeded along a new path, and the Cabinet learned of the change only a few days before the man on the street did. (O1) Another former official with more recent experience commented, "This is not my recollection of events. We felt obliged to let Cabinet know if we had changed our general assessment in significant degree." (D2)

Just as the influence of the Prime Minister probably increased in the last of the Trudeau years before May 1979, it is likely that the input of Cabinet increased too. The formal cabinet committee structure gave opportunities for other ministers to comment on economic matters that the old system did not afford. (M4) Once the Prime Minister started to ask searching questions relevant to the development of a budget, it would have been difficult to stop other ministers from following his lead. Perhaps of equal or greater importance would have been the decline in the defensive posture adopted by Finance. When the members of the Cabinet agreed that growth in expenditures had to be reduced to satisfy the voters, (D2) the adversarial relationship between Finance and the Treasury Board Secretariat on one side and all other departments on the other disappeared. (D2, M4) Co-operation being the watchword, Finance probably became more forthcoming. Personnel changes, both ministerial and official, also contributed to the new spirit of co-operation—a spirit that constituted a complete reversal of departmental traditions. (M3)

Parliament

The denouement of the revenue budget story can be briefly told. With the presentation of the budget to Cabinet, the executive-bureaucratic process has

---

[10] "The Fiscal Framework" includes budgetary revenues less budgetary expenditures plus nonbudgetary uses of funds—primarily loans and advances. The algebraic sum yields net cash requirements. A forecast of the fiscal framework for the coming fiscal year is included with each budget. In addition, since the early 1970s, the Cabinet is provided with periodic revisions of the fiscal framework during the year. When actual revenues differ from those previously forecast, inferences can be readily drawn. (D1, D2)

D1 Be careful; it is not so clear. Compare Sharp in early 1968.

D1 It depends to some extent [on] whether the wording of the amendment to the motion is a clear motion of no confidence in the government—or is accepted as such by the government.

D2 Not as I recall it, but you may have inside information. We certainly didn't construct a budget for the purpose of having it defeated!

almost been completed. On budget night around 8:00 p.m., the Minister of Finance has risen and moved, "That this House approves in general the budgetary policy of the Government." He then has given his budget speech, consisting normally of four parts:

1) a review of economic conditions and problems based on information from a White Paper tabled a few days earlier;

2) a statement of government revenues and expenditures over the past year and a comparison with the previous budget's estimations;

3) an estimation of government expenditures and revenues for the upcoming year and the surplus or deficit;[11] and

4) notice of any ways and means motions[12] —that is, motions to introduce bills to amend various tax acts.[13]

The budget debate has followed for up to six days. If the initial motion of the Minister has been defeated, (D1) or any significant amendments have been added, the government has fallen,[14] (D1) as occurred in May 1974 and in December 1979. The first defeat was probably engineered by the government (D2); the second most certainly was not.

Almost invariably, however, the motion has carried; and on chosen days after the debate, each ways and means motion has been introduced and voted upon, but not debated. Subsequently, the tax bills have been introduced into the House. After second reading—indicating approval of the purposes of the bills—they have been sent to a Committee of the Whole House for clause-by-clause consideration. Any amendments (not contrary to the general purpose of the bill) have been made at this stage. The Committee then has "reported" to the House where the bill (as a whole) has been give third reading and sent to the Senate. Few changes have occurred at either of the last two stages. The bills have become law after receiving Royal Assent.[15]

Overview

Few would deny the enormous importance to any government of changes in the tax system. These changes can affect significantly the range of expenditure

---

[11] The fiscal framework previously described.

[12] Giving notice of a ways and means motion enables the Minister of Finance to implement tax changes immediately. Since 1968, any Minister can, by a notice of a ways and means motion *without* the necessity of a budget debate, introduce a tax change. John Stewart, "The Tax Reform Bill in Parliament" (January-February 1971), 19 *Canadian Tax Journal* 1-7, at 3-4.

[13] Ibid., 3; and Robert J. Bertrand, Alice Desjardins, and René Hurtubise, *Legislation, Administration and Interpretation Processes in Federal Taxation,* Study for the Royal Commission on Taxation #22 (Ottawa: Queen's Printer, 1967), 63-64.

[14] Supra footnote 12, at 3.

[15] Ibid., 3-7.

D1   Why?

D1   But normally did not.

D1   A considerable part of the secrecy involved in the budget is the normal secrecy supposed to control government measures under consideration.

O1   The Finance role of critically scrutinizing the proposals of spending departments has been characterized by a former Deputy Minister as serving as the "internal opposition."

O2   Agreed.

M3   Agreed. The Prime Minister, when conflicts arose, frequently did not support his Minister of Finance or President of Treasury Board on expenditure restraint. This essentially led to a breakdown of the balance of power. The cabinet committee structure facilitated end runs of Finance and TBS and thereby a loss of expenditure control.

D1   I agree!

D2   I agree.

O3   Indeed, it was because of the omnipotence and secrecy of Finance that it so often lost fights on expenditure restraint. Lack of openness led to lack of cooperation.

M3   Most of the tax expenditure proposals came from cabinet committees.

options, the level of aggregate demand (inflation-employment-balance of payments), the structure of industry, and the distribution of income and wealth. On reflection, one cannot help being somewhat astonished (D1) that, at least until very recently, these policy changes were introduced unilaterally and preemptorily by the Minister of Finance and the Minister of National Revenue, who perforce were heavily dependent upon the advice of their senior departmental officials. Other ministers laboured hour after hour, week after week, year after year in Cabinet meetings fighting for approval of their policy proposals. The Minister of Finance could, (D1) in his budget speech, make policy changes of much greater importance—indeed, policy changes that, in effect, pre-empted those of his colleagues—without consultation or approval.[16]

The tradition of budget secrecy, (D1) the barrier of technical complexity, the confidence of the Prime Minister, cabinet solidarity, and party loyalty in the House also have meant that what the Minister and his officials have asked for they have got, with the rarest of exceptions. Even in the years preceding the spring election of 1979, consultation with Cabinet was kept to the generalities of the fiscal "stance." Because there was a consensus that there was no manoeuvring room, this consultation was of limited significance. Specific tax proposals were not put to Cabinet for approval, and tax change (tax expenditure) proposals made by other ministers were rebuffed.[17]

To explain the phenomenon in terms of organizational inertia or tradition is of little assistance, in my opinion. In the absence of prime ministerial direction to the contrary, undoubtedly Finance ministers and officials appointed to their respective posts quite naturally assumed that their territories were the same as those of their predecessors. Presumably, they believed it was in their personal interest and in the public interest to fight to maintain those territories. The Finance tradition is long, proud, and honourable, and worth perpetuating. The pre-emptive powers of the Minister/officials seldom, if ever, have been abused, and no doubt the preponderance of influence historically exercised by the Department has precluded innumerable follies (or worse) on the part of other ministers. Cabinets do need a countervailing force, if for nothing else, to protect the ministers from themselves as they pursue the often narrow interests for which they are responsible. (O1) A government can be as good as or better than the sum of the parts only if the appearance of balance

---

[16] Upon reading a draft of the text, a former senior Finance official made the following marginal comment:

This essay conveys an impression of an all-powerful Finance Department, having its way with the government. My impression is so different. It is one of a continuing fight with other departments to try to control their spending. [O2] A fight in which Finance could normally count only on Treasury Board [Secretariat] for support; a fight which, time and time again, was lost. [M3, D1, D2, O3]

[17] This observation also drew a response from the former official referred to supra footnote 16: "Nonsense! How did we ever build up all these tax expenditures?" (M3)

D2   Does this imply a significant shift after 1977? If that is intended, it is inaccurate.

M2   More accurately, of the public interest in the most general sense. I have never looked upon myself as an emanation of the Prime Minister, and I doubt [that] any of my successors did either.

M3   Nonsense. The Prime Minister failed me, particularly on the expenditure side.

O3   I am not sure things will be different with the Liberals.

M3   Untrue. The powers were if anything greater. The point is not a decline in the pre-emptive powers, but a reduced pressure from other ministers to increase expenditures, thus reducing the pressure on Finance. However, the earlier effects of the committees were to generate the deficit.

O2   This overview is accurate enough, but the reality was that it was simply the *business* of the Department of Finance to produce budgets. There were no other departments that aspired to this role, nor did any other group have the expertise to do it. My recollection is that other departments that had a cause—such as mining or petroleum incentives—could have a very strong influence, because in that case *they* were experts and were consulted.

O3   I would rephrase. Expenditure restraint forced ministers to demand a greater say in tax expenditures and in fiscal policy generally.

A3   1) There seems to be a tension between Finance's pre-emptive power and the widespread perception that the budgetary process is not under control. Perhaps this is because most of our perceptions of budgeting are shaped by the expenditure side, while Chapter 2 describes the revenue side, over which Finance may indeed have determinative clout. Even so, I would make more of factors which countervail Finance power, in the spirit of the. . .comments of the former Deputy included in the text. Perhaps you could draw upon David Good's imagery of anticipations: is it possible that Finance's pre-emption power is more apparent than real, in [that] Finance anticipates objections and incorporates them into proposals paraded as its own?

    2) The last paragraph is too compressed and thus is opaque. I wonder if a plausible summary of the points in the final paragraph would be the following:

    a) The enhanced cabinet committee structure created the organizational precondition for departmental resistance to Finance's pre-emptive powers.

    b) [From] 1968-1975: such resistance was unnecessary, however, as the growing revenue base and progressivity permitted the Department of Finance to yield in advance to anticipated tax expenditure demands; the very availability of Supply lessened pressures for tax expenditures anyway.

    c) Post-1975: indexation and the slowed growth in the revenue base simultaneously increased pressure for tax expenditures as a substitute for real expenditures and decreased the room for such concessions; these pressures are now transmitted with especial efficiency by the cabinet committee system. This closes the circle.

among the parts is maintained. Until 1977-1979, the Minister of Finance and the President of the Treasury Board were, in effect, emanations of the Prime Minister, (D2, M2, M3) constantly striving to put together an ever-changing bundle of coherent policies. Had the Clark administration survived, it is unlikely that the more powerful cabinet committee system put in place would have been willing to acquiesce in Finance's traditional pre-emptive tax policy changes. (O3)

The decline in the pre-emptive powers of the Department of Finance in the late 1970s reflected at least four simultaneous factors: perceived rising electoral hostility to "big government"; a series of large budget deficits that were treated as symptoms of irresponsibility and threats to price stability; the development of more powerful (and staffed) cabinet committees; and changes in personalities. (M3) Some of these factors may prove to be ephemeral. It remains to be seen whether ministers most of the time in most circumstances can effectively pursue their specific interests, while at the same time having adequate regard for the interest of the Cabinet as a collectivity and for the economy as a whole. (O2, O3, A3)

D1   One of the serious problems was the [change] in the timing of corporate tax payments and the options given corporate taxpayers to pay on previous year or estimated current year. However, the record is worrying.

D2   The main problem was the economic forecasting—including the rising inflation rate, which gave such a lift to revenue prior to indexing.

D1   Not necessarily.

M2   Is this really so? It needs more justification. The question is not whether the forecasting was accurate; that is a relatively insignificant matter compared [with] the question of whether or not the policy was in the right direction, over the long haul as well as the short haul.

D2   Many were [the] result of the basic and innovative changes introduced in tax reform.

M3   See earlier comment on the deliberate rollback of tax reform.

D1   And [they have] arisen from the efforts to make reform.

3

Appraisal and Evaluation

There have been a large number of complaints about the process of economic policy making in general and tax policy in particular. Many of the problems, however, are closely related to each other, and it is almost impossible to tell if one stems from another or if they originate from other sources altogether. In this chapter, the main problems are identified, primarily on the basis of the interviews of this study and those reported by David Good. Because some of the problems are self-explanatory, they are mentioned only briefly; others are set forth at greater length. The next chapter discusses the reforms that have been proposed by the interviewees and others.

Quality of Decision Making

Although few observers have questioned the competence of the Finance staff directly involved in economic policy making, the quality of some of the decisions came under fire from some of the interviewees. The strongest criticism was directed at the tendency of the Department to underestimate revenues in the earlier Trudeau era. As was mentioned in Chapter 1, by 1976 the forecasts had been low in 18 of 19 previous years. (D1, D2) In addition, the reliability of the Department's forecasts in all areas of economic analysis were questioned by none other than a former Deputy Minister of Finance. Poor forecasting performance would explain, of course, (D1) poor policy performance and hence, to some extent, the poor economic performance of the country. (M2) This important but difficult assessment issue is not pursued further here. The interested reader might consult W. Irwin Gillespie's recent article on the subject.[1]

On the tax structure side, a Canadian Tax Foundation report presented to the Finance Minister in 1977 criticized the increasing number of amendments that were necessary in recent budgets.[2] The reader will recall that in 1972 and 1973, 175 amendments were required; in 1974, 146 more were proposed; and in 1976, 75. (D2) These amendments have significantly increased complexity and uncertainty. (M3, D1)

---

[1] W. Irwin Gillespie, "Postwar Canadian Fiscal Policy Revisited 1945-1975" (May-June 1979), 27 *Canadian Tax Journal* 265-76.

[2] Tax Legislative Process Committee, "The Tax Legislative Process" (March-April 1978), 26 *Canadian Tax Journal* 157-81, at 172.

M4   The amendments are made frequently to meet the criticisms of Sherbaniuk, the CTF, and practitioners.

A3   Isn't this a by-product of tax expenditures?

D1   We had quite a lot of outside advice in 1967-1971, but we were attempting to make changes that broke new ground which the outside experts had not explored. Was it wrong to try?

D1   I don't think the problems of 1971 and 1972 really came from what you say here.

O1   The major reason for the complexity of tax legislation is not technical incompetence, as suggested, but rather the necessity of targeting tax expenditures to meet specific policy goals in a complex world.

M4   But the tax professions would not want sudden and final adoption of a bill that doesn't reflect special nuances that no official could possibly anticipate in advance.

M3   It's part of the democratic process.

D1   This is the result of the "open" part of the process. What would they feel if this preliminary planning too were open? They can't have it both ways.

Budget Complexity

Some observers claim that the budget is needlessly involved and complex.[3] (M4, A3) The CTF report pointed out that this affects not only lay observers; tax professionals as well spend an inordinate amount of time attempting to understand and keep up with the budget changes.[4] The increased number of amendments has tended to intensify this problem. To a large extent, the amendments have been needed because the Department, unable to obtain adequate outside advice at the outset, simply did not know what it was doing (or not doing) technically. (D1) The fundamental (D1) problem, however, arises from attempts to make fine distinctions in targeting tax concessions and incentives. It is beyond the scope of this study to attempt to appraise the effectiveness of these concessions: that the costs of understanding the tax structure have been raised enormously is beyond question. (O1)

In *The Hidden Costs of Taxation,* C. T. Sandford attempts to measure for Britain the costs of understanding budget measures.[5] One has only to consider the fees charged by tax advisers to recognize that these costs are not insignificant in Canada either.

Uncertainty

The CTF report also complained that although tax laws are normally in effect on budget day, they often do not receive Royal Assent for many months. In the interim, the legislation is subject to many amendments that may significantly affect some taxpayers. During the passage of the budget through Parliament, citizens are therefore in a state of limbo, uncertain as to the ultimate form of the legislation.[6] (M4) This uncertainty impedes private sector decision making. (M3, D1)

Tax Expenditures

The past decade has witnessed a plethora of new tax expenditures—the name given to taxes forgone in the provision of special concessions and incentives that would not be part of a neutral tax system. Because there is not unanimous agreement about the components of a neutral tax system, there is no agreed definition of a tax expenditure. Nevertheless, there is substantial agreement that many specific tax provisions do constitute tax expenditures and that these can be reliably estimated quantitatively and included with the bud-

---

[3] Ibid., 162, 172; and Douglas Sherbaniuk, "Budget Secrecy" (May-June 1976), 24 *Canadian Tax Journal* 223-30.

[4] Supra footnote 2, at 172, 173.

[5] C. T. Sandford, *The Hidden Costs of Taxation*, publication no. 6 (London: Institute for Fiscal Studies, 1973), ch. 3-5.

[6] Supra footnote 2, at 172.

D1   This is an improvement.

O2   Probably true—but how do you rule out people?

D2   All this says something about the quality of the interviewee! I don't agree. There are clear roles and responsibilities perceived and recognized regardless of personality.

D1   Naive.

M2   See my earlier comment on page 9.

D1   The selling of foreign exchange takes place very often. Sometimes it will help the budget. It would be unlikely the Department/Bank of Canada would sell much in the market for this purpose. The sale of foreign exchange from the exchange account to the Bank is often done for temporary financing and there would be normally no need to tell the Prime Minister. It shows up in the weekly statement of the assets and liabilities of the Bank.

D2   Nuts.

O2   Nonsense!

O2   Agreed.

D1   Very much so, and on the whole Canada has been lucky.

M2   Character may be less important than experience.

get.[7] Just before introducing the budget of December 11, 1979, the Department acceded to this request in order, no doubt, to discourage the demand for tax expenditures in a period of expenditure restraint. (D1)

Integration of Monetary and Fiscal Policy

One interviewee criticized the formal way in which monetary and fiscal policies have been integrated. The informality of the relationship between the Department of Finance and the Bank of Canada means, according to one of our interviewees, that the quality and amount of interaction are highly dependent on the personalities involved. (O2) This, he believes, has led to significant differences in the relationship. (D2) Another observer (D1) claimed that the lack of a formal method of integration has given the economic policy makers the opportunity to disguise their actions. (M2) He pointed to an incident in which the Department was selling foreign exchange to help finance the deficit without bothering even to inform the Prime Minister. (D1, D2, O2) The reader should, however, be aware that, as mentioned earlier, when the Canadian dollar is being supported (some days yes, some days no), Canadian dollars are purchased. These transactions are public knowledge every month, so that an attempt to conceal them from the Prime Minister would be silly. And surely the Prime Minister would not wish to be kept informed on an hour-to-hour basis!

Dependence on Personalities

One of the difficulties in writing about the changing role of the Department of Finance is that personalities, like circumstances, alter cases. An organization's style and substance can vary greatly with the personalities involved. A Prime Minister, after an election, can bring about major changes in both procedure and distribution of responsibility. Even within the Department of Finance, with all its traditions, the addition or subtraction of one or two individuals can effect appreciable differences in the way the Department operates and in the decisions that emerge. (O2)

Obviously, much depends on the personality of the Finance Minister. (D1) As has been seen, each Minister has had his own unique sources of information. Obviously, too, the influence of these sources has varied from Minister to Minister. In addition, the character (M2) and capabilities of the individual

---

[7]David A. Good, "The Politics of Anticipation" (Ph.D. dissertation, University of California, Berkeley, 1979), 172, 363ff; Alan Maslove, "The Other Side of Public Spending," in G. Bruce Doern and Alan M. Maslove, eds., *The Public Evaluation of Government Spending* (Montreal: Institute for Research on Public Policy, 1978), 149-68; and Denis Smith, "President and Parliament: The Transformations of Parliamentary Government in Canada," in T. A. Hockin, ed., *The Apex of Power: The Prime Minister and Political Leadership in Canada*, 2nd ed. (Scarborough, Ont.: Prentice-Hall, 1977), 308-25.

O2   R. Bryce.

O2   Simon Reisman!

O1   Distinction between the advocate type of Deputy Minister and the zealot type is highly artificial. Most deputies would probably exhibit both of these characteristics to varying degrees.

D2   On the contrary, we began the more formal exchanges of information—perhaps because we had to.

M2   Proof? Is the inference that deputy ministers would be questioned on the advice they had given to their ministers?

M3   What does this mean? The Minister is accountable, and he should be able to control his Deputy or replace him.

D1   They are very accountable to their Minister and through him (and Michael Pitfield) to the Prime Minister.

D2   Interdepartmentally, most of the consultation has to proceed at all levels—from most junior officers up to assistant deputy ministers. [The] Prime Minister and Simon Reisman expected us all to consult and keep in touch.

Minister dictate how much of his own officials' advice he will accept at face value.

Of equal and, in some circumstances, greater importance is the incumbent of the position of Deputy Minister. David Good distinguished two types of deputies. One was an advocate type (a more descriptive term would be "conciliator"), (O2) who tended to promote wide discussion and debate on issues within the Department. Rather than make unilateral decisions, he would attempt to bring his assistant deputy ministers to a consensus. Decisions were usually arrived at slowly but carefully under this type of Deputy Minister. The second type Good identified was the zealot. (O2) The zealot tended to work at a much faster pace and have much firmer opinions than the advocate. At meetings with his officials, he would attempt to bring them around to his way of thinking rather than reach a compromise.[8]   (O1)

The very character of the Department as a whole may depend on the Deputy Minister. One participant in meetings of the federal-provincial Continuing Committee on Fiscal and Economic Matters noted that during the 1960s the federal Department of Finance had become considerably more open. With the appointment of Simon Reisman as Deputy Minister in April 1970, it seemed to become close-mouthed again. Other observers too have noted a reluctance in the Department to consult as freely when Reisman was the Deputy. (D2) While the lack of consultation, in itself, poses problems, the problem is intensified when interested parties are unable to predict how the attitude of the Department will change when its head changes. Because the Department is made up of men, and because men are different, it is difficult to see a solution to the dependence on personality, with one important proviso: the concern about personality would be greatly reduced if either the authority of the incumbents were reduced and/or they, directly or indirectly, were held more accountable (M2) for the exercise of that authority. (M3, D1, D2)

Jurisdictional Disputes

In the past, the Department of Finance was pre-eminent in the provision of economic advice and in the implementation of financial, tax structure, and stabilization policies. Even the development and/or reorganization of other departments (such as Industry, Trade and Commerce, Regional Economic Expansion, and Energy, Mines and Resources) did not, at least initially, significantly change this position. Some observers claimed that many of the problems in the policy-making process in the past decade or so resulted from attempts by Finance to maintain power and influence despite the Department's waning capacity relative to the increasing magnitude of the task and the growing competence of others. They believed that the consistent underestimation

---

[8] *Supra* footnote 7, Good.

D2   Baloney.

D2   You might make a case if this is directed at tax policy matters only.

O1   It is misleading and incorrect to suggest that Finance intentionally under-estimated revenues to maintain jurisdictional territory. All efforts have been made to produce unbiased forecasts. The period covered by the study, 1962-1979, was characterized by rising inflation. In this sort of environment, there is a natural tendency to underestimate inflation and nominal income growth and thus tax revenues. In addition, following tax reform there was a period in which labour income was underestimated and had to be consistently revised upward. This also caused revenue to be underestimated for a time. It was followed by a period in which revenue was overestimated because of an exaggerated notion of the elas-ticity of the reformed tax system stemming from comparisons of actual personal tax revenue growth with the downward biased tax base. It should be stressed that forecast errors did not result from strategic considerations. They were simply honest errors.

D1   At times.

D1   You should say more about this and what the issues are. It has always been felt that the Department of [Industry,] Trade and Commerce is too close to the industries [it] "serves" and therefore biased toward protectiveness. External has never wanted to get into the messy details of tariffs, but would and had a voice in general policy ever since N. A. Robertson got involved in the 1932 conference in Ottawa.

O2   Agreed.

D2   I disagree completely. As I observed it, the Prime Minister was incredibly attentive to the concerns of individual ministers.

M2   In my view, the powers of the PCO have been exaggerated. What is true is that the power and influence of most senior officials [have] been reduced be-cause of the formalization of procedures.

D2   I disagree. If anything, I think our influence, if not power, has increased.

D2   I welcomed this; it made our job much easier and economic policy more coherent.

M2   Just as the Minister of Agriculture would have resisted a similar group of farm representatives in the Prime Minister's office advising on agriculture policies. The Prime Minister has to have confidence in his ministers, otherwise the system does not work. The Minister of Finance can, of course, be downgraded by the appointment of a super economic minister, but that hasn't been an overwhelm-ing success where it has been tried!

M3   I handled this myself.

of revenues, (D2) the overdevotion to budget secrecy, and the exclusion of cabinet input have been deliberately used by the Department to maintain its jurisdictional territory. (D2, O1) Certainly, this situation has not been accepted gracefully by all members of the government. Power struggles have arisen as other agencies have questioned the right of the Department to its domain and have made sorties across its borders.

Traditionally, there has been (D1) jealousy among the Department of Finance, Industry, Trade and Commerce, and External Affairs over the right to determine tariffs, for example. (D1, O2) In the earlier Trudeau era, for the reasons discussed earlier, serious challenges to the pre-eminence of Finance came from entirely different sources: the further development and formalization of the cabinet committee system and the greatly expanded PCO secretariat. Some claimed at the time that with Mr. Trudeau prime ministerial and parliamentary government had become a presidential and republican government.[9] (D2) The greater emphasis on formalized decision-making processes and long-range planning, coupled with a greatly expanded PCO support staff, accompanied the shift from individual ministerial responsibility to nominally collective, but in fact centralized, responsibility. (M2) This resulted in reduced power and influence for most senior officials, including Finance officials,[10] but excluding, of course, the senior officials of the PCO. (D2)

The advent of what was ostensibly "collegial" government but was actually highly centralized government created, many have felt, a vacuum in the decision-making process. One former Minister even claimed that the collective decision-making process had led only to confusion and, ironically, a lack of forward planning and coherence.[11]

The Department of Finance did not submit meekly to the reduction of its traditional jurisdiction. While Finance officials were able to say little about Mr. Trudeau maintaining his own personal economic advisers, such as Albert Breton and Ian Stewart, (D2) they reacted strongly against any attempt to institutionalize a system of competing economic advice. (M2) In 1974, when Albert Breton attempted to set up the ill-fated "group of seven" (a collection of experts who were to provide economic advice to the Prime Minister), the Department of Finance rebelled. Simon Reisman, along with a few other influential deputy ministers, threatened to resign unless the responsibility of Finance as the government's sole economic adviser was maintained. (M3) The group was then forced to disband.[12]

---

[9] Supra footnote 7, Smith.

[10] D. G. Hartle, *The Expenditure Budget Process in the Government of Canada*, Canadian Tax Papers no. 60 (Toronto: Canadian Tax Foundation, 1978), 5-7, and information obtained in interviews.

[11] Ibid., 7, and interviews.

[12] Ibid.

D2   But individual ministers and deputies continued to fight for larger shares of the constant pie, and we had to fight this just as rigorously.

M4   Remember that from mid-1975 to 1978 there were wage and price controls. The role of fiscal policy was to a degree supplemented by the direct instrument.

M3   They were co-opted.

M2   [Mr.] Chrétien, however, refused to become a member of the Board of Economic Development Ministers, thus retaining his authority on fiscal and monetary policy, which is his direct responsibility.

D2   We were always anxious to support moves to improve co-ordination and consistency among departments as well as with our own macropolicy.

O3   No.

D2   Not by me. We talked daily on the phone, lunched with martinis frequently, exchanged information and perceptions all through the piece, and as a result influence flowed in both directions.

D1   Borrowing operations apart from Treasury Bill issues always required some approval, but monetary policy never did except for changes in par value, etc.

D1   More debt management strategy was needed then.

M3   I think the criticisms are overblown. If the Minister had a more open door policy, the problem would largely disappear.

The last third of the Trudeau era was different in some respects and similar in others. It was different inasmuch as government expenditure and employment restraint were unanimously accepted, (D2) with the result that Finance could suspend its adversarial role vis-à-vis most of the departments and ministers. (M4) It was different in that personalities changed: Michael Pitfield was then Secretary to the Cabinet; Messrs. Turner and Reisman were replaced by Messrs. Macdonald/Chrétien and Shoyama/Hood. Mr. Shoyama was much more the conciliator than was Mr. Reisman, as was Mr. Macdonald as compared with Mr. Turner. Mr. Pitfield convened meetings of the so-called economic deputies. After some "to-ing" and "fro-ing," Mr. Shoyama became the chairman. When political imperatives required the creation of the Board of Economic Development Ministers, the bureaucratic groundwork had, in a sense, been laid. Neither Mr. Chrétien nor Mr. Shoyama actively resisted the move, (M3) although it clearly meant a further reduction in what had once been Finance's preponderance of influence in structural economic questions. (M2, D2)

But there were similarities too. Ian Stewart, an economic adviser to the Prime Minister at the time and later Deputy Minister of Finance, had increasing influence with the Prime Minister on matters economic. (O3) This was resented as "second guessing": (D2) Finance still cherished what it believed to be its right to a monopoly of the role of economic adviser. Another constancy, until recently, was Finance's refusal to relinquish its pre-emptive roles with respect to tax and financial policy. In earlier years, Finance did not seek prior cabinet approval of tax structure changes, nor did it obtain prior approval of the debt management/monetary policies it pursued. (D1) In and subsequent to the Macdonald-Shoyama/Hood era, however, cabinet documents seeking approval of debt management strategy (D1') went forward regularly, and any deviation from the agreed pattern was drawn explicitly to the attention of ministers.

The Clark government's continuation and extension of the cabinet committee structure to include an official inner cabinet and staff support for the Economic Development (the former BEDM) and Social Policy committees did nothing to resolve the jurisdictional problem. Perhaps these developments even intensified it.

Budget Secrecy

Of all the complaints about the development and implementation of economic policy through a budget, the most common is the attack on the pervasive influence of budget secrecy. (M3) The tradition of secrecy originally developed when budgets were used only as means of financing government programs. It was feared that advance knowledge of budgetary measures might give a few individuals an unfair opportunity either to avoid a financial loss or to realize a financial gain. Now, however, budgets play a much more extensive role in economic, social, and political matters. Consequently, they are immensely more complicated. Moreover, foreknowledge of most income tax changes

D1   Some of the changes in corporate and business taxes would.

D1   But then much is needed to make it effectively open to all.

D1   But information on most government policy measures under consideration is supposed to be withheld.

D1   But decisions on many regulatory matters are also secret until announced, even "exposure drafts."

D2   See my comments on page 17.

D1   When a decision in general terms or in principle has been reached, there can be very detailed and controversial discussions of it. For example, Jim Brown and I had a series of very difficult and bitter discussions with a committee of presidents of the life insurance companies about how, and how much, we were going to tax them in 1938.

M2   Have they done so on budgetary tax changes, for example?

D1   Usually? Only their views of federal policies.

D1   This related to our discussion of possible *changes* in the White Paper. The provinces were expressing views and asking questions about federal intentions.

M2   I would be surprised if provincial finance ministers broke their pledges of budgetary secrecy.

D2   Not so unless this refers to tax changes; and if so, it is distorted. We would receive information only about income tax changes under the tax collection agreements. This was necessary for administrative purposes. But provinces never divulged their own plans for tax changes other than as required for the collection arrangements.

APPRAISAL AND EVALUATION   40

would provide no opportunity for private gain. (D1) Both insiders and outsiders alike have demanded, not surprisingly, a re-examination of the role of
secrecy. It is almost universally believed that the complexities of most structural tax changes necessitate more open consultation on both the technical
and the impact aspects. (D1)

Indeed, aside from commodity tax changes, there is some question as to
whether there is any need for withholding information on budget matters.
The issue is, of course, not the budget, per se, but insider information on any
matter that can be used for personal gain. (D1) Prior knowledge of a regulatory
decision can be just as valuable as prior knowledge of a sales tax change,[13] for
example. (D1)

The reticence of the Department of Finance has led to fairly significant
problems for outsiders. David Good claims that the need for silence has led to
the development of what he calls "the politics of anticipation." Rather than
discuss options with interested parties, Finance officials have carefully observed
the views and past behaviour of interested parties and have anticipated how
they would react to the proposed measures. They have, in other words, seldom
been surprised. This tactic has resulted in complaints about the seeming non-
response of the Department to briefs. Supplicants have become frustrated
with the lack of feedback from Finance on their views. They have had no way
of knowing whether their views have been seriously considered. The lack of a
public forum—Parliament being dismissed as ineffective in this area—in which
to express and debate opinions on various issues has caused informed members
of the public to feel that there has been inadequate pressure on Finance to
justify the policy choices made. Finance officials, on the other hand, have
been reluctant to comment on any issue for fear of "tipping their hand" and
divulging how they have felt about issues.[14] (D2) Perhaps too, on occasion,
they have sought to avoid unpleasant confrontations and/or revelations of
ignorance. Furthermore, *in principle,* the feelings and beliefs of officials are
irrelevant: the officials are advisers to ministers, not decision makers. Only
the Minister can properly argue with those presenting briefs. (D1)

Provinces have been especially critical of the traditional reticence of the
federal Department of Finance. Provincial officials have felt that while they
have been willing to divulge information on their own policies, (M2, D1) the
federal government has not reciprocated in kind. In an interview, a former
Deputy Minister of Finance recognized this problem. While he regretted the
situation, he claimed that budget secrecy made silence necessary.[15] (D1) Presumably, the provinces could have used precisely the same argument had they
chosen to do so.   (M2, D2)

---

13 Robert J. Bertrand, Alice Desjardins, and René Hurtubise, *Legislation, Administration and Interpretation Processes in Federal Taxation,* Study for the Royal Commission
on Taxation #22 (Ottawa: Queen's Printer, 1967), 44-49.

14 More detail can be found in all the sources cited previously in this chapter.

15 Robert Bryce, quoted in supra footnote 3, at 226.

D1   You are accountable afterward, surely.

O1   Budget secrecy does not necessarily reduce the accountability of government. When the Minister presents his budget, he does justify his choices of tax measures to the public. He does this in the speech itself, in the budget debate, in the clause-by-clause consideration of the bill by the Committee of the Whole, in his interviews with the media, and in other contacts with the public. In addition, in recent years the Minister has been releasing a great deal of background material along with the budget. The December 11, 1979 budget with its several discussion papers is a prime case in point. Also, it is not true that the public, including Parliament, is often not in a position to provide informed criticisms of the budget. There is a budget lock-up for MPs and another for the media at which officials are present to answer questions. In addition, the main measures in some recent budgets have not caught the public entirely by surprise and thus there has been significant debate of such proposals as manufacturer's sales tax cuts, retail sales tax cuts, the mortgage interest and property tax credit, and the excise tax on transportation fuels prior to their introduction. The process of budget preparation has been opening up to a singificant degree.

D1   They have time later.

D2   For example, indexing, fast write-off, refundable credits, 25 per cent cut in general sales tax, dividend tax index—he's quite wrong.

D1   "Distant distillations" of intragovernment gossip.

D2   Nonsense. My predecessors always welcomed a new idea or a sharp debate, and I learned, I hope, from them.

O2   Certainly not so in my day—there [were] constant and relevant arguments among officials on many aspects of policy.

M2   Perhaps it is different now. When I was an official in the Department of Finance, the debate was spirited, even occasionally before the Minister. I encouraged such debate when later I myself became Minister.

D2   More nonsense.

D1   Lots of things *may* happen.

D1   Do you think Simon Reisman or Thomas Shoyama would tolerate [his] officers behaving this way?

D2   Good didn't interview me. I couldn't disagree more with his thesis.

O1   It is not true that there is not a healthy internal debate prior to the budget. Officials are not as reluctant to express their views as you suggest.

D1   The problem is to consult fully openly. As noted elsewhere, there is a general code of secrecy about government decisions while they are under consideration, but something can be done by publishing Green Papers and White Papers.

D2   Claptrap!

From an outsider's viewpoint, the primary disadvantage of budget secrecy is that it tends to lessen the accountability of the government. (D1, O1) The Department appears arbitrary, if not capricious. In receiving suggestions as it has done, the Department has appeared simply to pick and choose options without justifying the choice. As well, without prior debate on budget measures, the public (including Parliament) is often not in a position to provide informed criticism when the measures are announced. (D1)

Extreme secrecy has some adverse effects on the Department itself. Officials have complained that they have been unable to solicit information on some issues for fear of exposing intentions. Finance ministers, particularly, have felt hampered, explaining that the current conditions leave them heavily dependent on their Department's advice. The result has been the adoption of other tactics to compensate for this lack of information.

Good distinguishes three different techniques:

1) incrementalism: the hedging against uncertainty by implementing only incremental measures; (D2)

2) assessing the political climate: usually a "seat of the pants" judgment from within the Department; and

3) dependence on the mutual trust of participants: the need to rely on the judgments and abilities of other colleagues.[16]

Although all three tactics have been effective in a limited sense, Good attacks the last one in particular. The need to develop trust within the bureaucracy—both to prevent disagreement that might lead to a breaking of the code of silence, and to encourage co-operation and eliminate duplication of work—has led to a sort of internal "politics of anticipation." Rather than explicitly state his views, the "typical" official has first tested the waters to determine where his colleagues or his superiors have stood. (D1) If their views have appeared to be significantly different from his own, the official normally has modified his view so that open disagreement cannot result. This approach has precluded "healthy" debate, (D2, O2, M2) and it can be argued that too often the resultant policies have tended to lack creativity and even foresight. Another problem has been a tendency on the part of subordinates to recommend only those policies with results that are easily predictable. (D2) As Good says, an official eager to gain or maintain the trust of his superior may (D1) be willing to sacrifice creative risk taking for unimaginative certainty.[17] (D1, D2, O1) This problem does not stem only from budget secrecy, of course; it is probably endemic to all bureaucratic decision making. It is not without virtue: it makes for an extremely stable system. Budget secrecy, however, intensifies the problem. The degree of reliance on mutual trust would not be so urgent if the Department could more freely consult sources outside the government. (D1, D2)

---

[16] Supra footnote 7, Good, at 42-98.

[17] Ibid., passim, but particularly 348-51, and information obtained in interviews.

D1   One of the problems in the tax field is that there is little argument pro and con from those outside; it is nearly always the interested parties against the government.

M2   That is what officials would be bound to say! In fact and truthfully, they are also sensitive to the Minister's political concerns and do not make a habit of offering unacceptable advice.

D1   This is the usual textbook distinction, but good senior officials can and will argue the political aspects of proposals (not the clearly partisan or constituency arguments), and ministers appreciate hearing their views if they are sensible in substance and manner.

D2   Does this suggest that officials paid no attention to political needs and imperatives? If so, it's obviously wrong.

D1   Outside observers.

D1   Where it is directly between the two of them, it is obvious they will be careful and secretive.

M1   This description tends to overplay potential conflicts between [the] Prime Minister and Minister of Finance. There [are] more likely to be conflicts between other ministers and the Finance Minister that the Prime Minister is called upon to settle, and he is almost bound to support the Minister of Finance.

D1   There were a number of meetings of the Minister and Deputy Minister of Finance and L. B. Pearson and Tom Kent—with some real debate.

D2   How does he know?

Accountability

The pre-eminent role played by the Department of Finance in some policy fields has led observers to question how accountable it actually has been, both to the Executive and to Parliament. What political controls have there been on the Department? The description of the production of a revenue budget in Chapter 2 showed the roles of the various actors in the process. Let us now briefly re-examine their roles to see what influence the Finance Minister, the Prime Minister, Cabinet, and Parliament exert in the economic policy decision-making process. (D1)

There has been little criticism of the relationship between the Minister of Finance and his Department. David Good described the relationship as one in which the officials supplied technical and professional expertise and the Minister provided political input.[18] (M2, D1, D2) Our own interviews confirmed this and emphasized the fact that former ministers believe that they made the final decisions on *all* major departmental matters. Although one cannot avoid the suspicion that the relationship must have been strained on some issues, all parties seem to agree that the proper situation has prevailed.

The past influence of the Prime Minister is less obvious. The "politics of anticipation" make it almost impossible for observers (D1) to determine who plays the most significant role in coming to a decision. As we have seen, the relationship between the Finance Minister and the Prime Minister has been, above all, one of anticipation. Neither has wished to allow a divergence of opinion to develop into an actual disagreement. Instead, they probably have let contentious issues drop temporarily until one or the other or both have modified their stands. It is, therefore, virtually impossible to decide who has given away the most to the other. (D1) (M1)

David Good claims that the Prime Minister's influence has been on the "most macro-level."[19] (D1, D2) Although on some pressing economics-related issues—energy, for instance—the Prime Minister may have become closely involved, Good's claim probably has been valid for the revenue budget and most other stabilization policy decisions. Nevertheless, as just discussed, in the final years of the previous Trudeau administration, the Prime Minister almost certainly had a greater influence than in the late 1960s and early 1970s.

The tactics of anticipation also make it almost impossible to determine the extent of the Cabinet's role in the decision-making process. Officials pointed out in our interviews that the Department has been well aware of the views of the Cabinet—through their own participation in cabinet committee meetings—and that its views were taken into account. Nonetheless, with the few exceptions where individual ministers were consulted on politically sensitive issues,

---

[18] Ibid., 289-92.
[19] Ibid., 299.

D1   Tax structure decisions normally require a degree of knowledge of the income tax law and concepts that very few ministers have. We had to teach them some for tax reform purposes.

D2   I disagree. They were put up for discussion and debate, as well as for information.
M2   Portfolios(?).

M2   Ministers of Finance, as well as other ministers, are expected to make proposals for consideration by their colleagues. They do not usually ask: what should I do?

O1   Parliamentary input was also made in response to the Commodity Tax Review Report.
D2   Not at all. The main difficulty is the extremely partisan and adversarial nature of the situation, making for rhetorical distortion and half-truths.

D1   Right, and it is for this reason I would favour referring tax bills—and Green or White Papers—to a Standing Committee.

D2   But they can seek changes in specific measures.
D1   This is an exaggeration. A particular bill, even an unimportant one, can be rejected, as long as it is not clearly a "want of confidence motion." Recall Sharp in early 1968.

it appears that the Cabinet as a whole has had little influence on some crucial economic policy issues (for example, tax structure and government finance). (D1) Informed of a budget's contents only a day or two before it is brought down, the Cabinet has had only two choices: either to accept the budget, with very minor modifications, or to demand significant changes that would result in its postponement. Because the latter choice would be almost suicidal, politically, inevitably the Cabinet has accepted the budget. In a similar manner, Finance's quarterly economic reports have been presented to Cabinet, not as subjects for debate, but as "for your information" documents. (D2) It may be that, given the nature of the individuals involved and their special interests, this situation is inescapable. (M2) If ministers were to have a greater say on decisions that could significantly affect the amount of money available to finance expenditures, the growth of these expenditures might well be even greater than it has been. Once again, though, the amount of cabinet input seems to have increased in the later years of the Trudeau administration up to May 1979. There is some evidence that the Cabinet Committee on Priorities and Planning began to play a much more substantive role, particularly in the development of the stance of the revenue budget. But did the Committee have more influence, or were there no options from which to choose? (M2)

The lack of accountability to Parliament is a result of many of the problems we have identified. The stringent budget secrecy constraint has precluded, with the exception of the Tax Reform White Paper, parliamentary input prior to the commitment of a government to a course of action. (O1) When the budget is presented to the House, the matters dealt with are often so complex as to preclude (D2) constructive criticism from members of Parliament. Usually, members are not sufficiently well informed to mount a forceful attack on the government's economic tax policies. The fact that budget measures are considered only in the Committee of the Whole House—eliminating the opportunity to hear witnesses—intensifies this problem. (D1)

Perhaps the greatest barrier to a more significant role for Parliament, though, is the drastic consequences of a budget failing to receive majority support in the House. If Parliament rejects a government's budget, the government falls. This fact ensures that government MPs will invariably support a budget; and, in a minority situation, some opposition members may be induced to support it to avoid an election, (D2) the Conservative defeat of December 1979 notwithstanding. (D1)

Accountability is a motherhood virtue: it is impossible to reject accountability as a goal. Nevertheless, it is possible to point out that the concept has no simple or obvious application when used in the context of "economic management." Accountability presumably means that the performance of those in authority is objectively assessed. Were the assigned responsibilities met as fully as the delegated powers and authority permitted? If said quickly, this sounds straightforward enough. Here are the widely accepted goals of economic policy: full employment, stable prices, optimal economic rate of

D2 And in Canada don't forget "regional balance"!

M2 Apart from the fact that Parliament is organized along partisan lines and the opposition will criticize whatever the government proposes, good or bad.

D2 How about the no-growth conservers?

growth, an equitable distribution of income. One could then parade the numbers for Canada each year and require the Department to justify the fact that the unemployment rate was over 4 per cent, the inflation rate over 1 per cent, the rate of growth of output less than 5 per cent; as for the distribution of income. . . .(D2) A moment's reflection, however, reveals that the goals are, to an uncertain and probably changing degree, in conflict with one another. When trade-offs are operative, it is not clear that such targets are mutually consistent. Nor is it clear what optimal departmental policies could have achieved. What fraction of the problem(s) was unsolvable within the prevailing constraints?

And come to think of it, what were those constraints? Could the Department have imposed wage, price, and exchange controls? Conscripted labour? Expropriated producers? Withdrawn unemployment insurance benefits for the young and for married women? Introduced rationing? Imposed force savings? One could go on. Few would deny that more accountability is better than less. But few of those knowledgeable about economic policy would deny that achieving accountability in this policy area is fraught with horrendous analytic, measurement, and ideological problems.   (M2)

The "equitable distribution of income" goal was mentioned above among the other economic goals, as though it were like the others, but it is not. There is little agreement about what the distribution of income is now, much less what it should be. Nor is there agreement about the effects of particular policies on other goals. There is, however, an even more profound difficulty related to the interpersonal allocation of income.

There is a wide measure of agreement about vague goals like full employment without inflation coupled with substantial economic growth. (D2) But the consensus is superficial in an important sense. Everyone can agree on the pursuit of the goals, except when he finds it in his own self-interest to act in ways that are antithetical to their realization. Economists emphasize, and rightly so, the desirability of policies that increase the size of the pie of goods and services. They pay scant regard to the distribution of those goods and services, arguing that with more available no one need have less. It is a fact of life, however, that individuals, directly or indirectly, press for personal advantages even if this means less for others. Indeed, they are often (usually?) willing to press for a relatively small personal advantage, even if it means a large disadvantage to others. In short, policy making in general and economic policy making in particular are inescapably fraught with conflict. The interests of individuals are not identical. The role of government is not only to do what everyone wants to be done, but somehow or other to resolve these endless conflicts.

To be more specific, most voters want more transfer payments for themselves and lower taxes for themselves. They want better public services with someone else paying for them. They want monopoly power for themselves by

M2   May I add that in Parliament the opposition is less concerned to improve the legislation placed before it by the government than it is to demonstrate the government's incompetence. Read Hansard and you will find it difficult to discern any difference between degree of criticism of measures that proved to be constructive and those that proved to be inept.

D1   I think it is desirable that ministers defend their general macroeconomic advice, before cabinet committees and in public before parliamentary committees. However, it is desirable [that] this should not be tied into budget proposals which the Minister has decided upon, because his prestige within the Cabinet is then at stake and that is very important.

dint of government regulation if necessary, but they also want government regulation to reduce the monopoly power of others. They want to sell with tariff protection and buy with free trade. The list is endless. Not only do they want these kinds of advantages, but they will vote for the party that promises them. And they will either lobby for the advantages themselves or pay others to do so. Parties are elected in part because their potential ministers of Agriculture, Labour, Industry, and so on are expected to deliver more advantages to special-interest groups than are those of competing parties. Somehow or other these interests are continually reconciled in a dynamic series of compromises. The "economic management" task is to achieve this reconciliation at the lowest possible cost to the collective interest—the collective interest captured in part by the well-known stability-growth goals of economic policy.

From this perspective, how would one assess the quality of the decisions of the Department of Finance? We can leave aside decisions based on faulty information and/or analysis: all can agree that these were unfortunate if less faulty data and analyses were attainable. But what about the others (pretending that these can be identified)? In the economic and political circumstances that prevailed at a particular time, would it have been better had the conflict been resolved differently? Presumably, there would have been less concern for some narrow interests and more concern for the collective interest. This in turn implies, however, that one is prepared to make judgments about the likelihood of a different reconciliation bringing about the defeat of a political party and about the ramifications of such an eventuality. Clearly, this goes far beyond the conventional notion of accountability.   (M2, D1)

Summary

Supporters of the Department of Finance would argue that it has been remarkably successful in gauging the wind and producing decisions that reconciled conflict. They would also argue, one would expect, that the Department has done good works by stealth—protecting the collective interest against special interests, with, for the most part, minimal concessions to the politically expedient. Critics, on the other hand, would argue that Finance officers, in order to preserve and enhance their power, have exploited budget secrecy, parliamentary rules and procedures, and cabinet tradition, so as to maintain the Department's pre-emptive powers with respect to decisions about the tax structure and government finance (to mention only two). The critics would further claim that many decisions of great moment that are binding on the government have been promulgated apparently without either informed advice or more than perfunctory prime ministerial or cabinet approval. These critics would no doubt go on to claim that the decisions issuing from the Department have been of lower quality than they needed to be under a more open system, and that a consequent cost has been imposed on the economy.

D1 I don't think you give sufficient attention to the great difficulty in reaching the right macroeconomic policies in the past decade of inflation-cum-unemployment. The fact is (in my view, and I am speaking of the time after I left) that the expert economists inside and outside the government have not had adequate understanding of the process and problems of inflation and therefore of the extent by which they must be accepted as a constraint upon the Keynesian analysis (or monetarist, too) in determining fiscal policy. In fact, the western world is going through a very difficult period (most of the communist world too), and there really is no assurance that "the human prospect" is a good one. The trouble with the Department of Finance is that [it has] to grapple with these very broad, and perhaps insoluble and painful, issues about which informed and able intellectuals can and do differ. In these times, I guess we do need a philosopher king, but it is too bad that they seem to become arrogant as time goes on rather than acknowledging the real difficulties of deciding what makes sense. Openness is not an answer in itself in these circumstances.

As was stated earlier, this paper will not attempt the impossible task of assessing objectively the overall performance of the Department over the past 10 to 15 years. In many respects, such an assessment is irrelevant. The critics are unlikely to be convinced by a favourable assessment, or the Department's defenders by an unfavourable one. Moreover, the pursuit of the strategems I have described is consistent both with the hypothesis that the Cabinet has to be protected from itself (or if you like, the voters protected from the Cabinet) *and* with the hypothesis that the officers are pursuing their self-interest at the expense of the collective interest. Here again, there is no objective basis for rejecting one hypothesis and accepting the other, nor is there much likelihood of changing the minds of those who are already convinced on the question. Quite possibly, both are partly valid and mutually reinforcing.

Rightly or wrongly, many of the Finance policies of the past decade are discredited in the eyes of the people who count, as is the decision-making process from which they have emerged. If it is difficult to assess objectively the quality of the earlier policies in terms of what was feasible rather than what was expected, it is impossible to determine the extent to which process failure explains policy failure. But this too is largely irrelevant. Had there been no perceived policy failure, the process would not be under attack. But even this is uncertain, for some object to the old process as elitist or undemocratic or authoritarian.

Certainly, when a process that is considered grievously flawed is associated with flawed policies, the demands for changes in the process are made more stridently and are more compelling to those seeking answers. The defenders of the old process are reduced to trying to explain how much worse the policies would have been had the process been more open, etc., etc. Their arguments are hardly persuasive, although conceivably valid, when the old process can be viewed as self-serving for those who were a part of it.

From this perspective, the next chapter reviews many of the proposals for process reform that have been advanced in recent years.   (D1)

D1   There are many informed spokesman inside, and some outside, the public service.

O1   It is going a bit too far to say that Finance has maintained a virtual monopoly on informed advice on stabilization. The Economic Council has been providing informed advice for quite some time. In addition, there has been a virtual flowering of research groups with a greater or lesser interest in stabilization policy. These groups include the Conference Board, the Howe Research Institute, Data Resources Incorporated, the Institute for Research on Public Policy, the Institute for Policy Analysis, and the Canadian Institute for Economic Policy. The contributions of these groups have helped to raise the tone of the public debate on stabilization policy issues.

M2   Would its recommendations be public or only for internal use?

D1   The Lambert proposal was essentially [related to] economic projections and revenue projections, not budget proposals. It contemplated expenditure plans, but I think this may be unrealistic in any detail at all—what government would want to disclose its decisions this way?

M2   And go to the roots of our parliamentary system of government, which is partisan and adversary.

D1   With this, I agree.

D1   The recent budgets have had more explanation.

4

Proposals for Reform

The budgetary process has not been without its critics. Indeed, complaints have been increasing both inside and outside the government.[1] The proposals for reform that have been advanced can be divided into three categories: pre-budget, budget, and post-budget reform.

Pre-budget reform primarily entails changing the current situation in which the Department of Finance has maintained a virtual monopoly on informed internal advice on stabilization and tax structure policy. (D1, O1) Reforms in this category therefore deal less with a direct change in the budgetary process itself than with changing the process of continuing analysis. This is the basis for the many recommendations that a permanent advisory and investigatory body be created, to perform a parallel and in a sense competitive role to that of Finance officials in the area of economic analysis, evaluation, and advice. (M2) Some critics who promote the establishment of a public fiscal framework go even further, advocating that a permanent, staffed economic policy parliamentary committee be established that would come close to having some government decision-making powers, and certainly would be part of the ongoing process.[2] (D1) The reforms in this category are the most far-reaching, for they seek to affect not just the production of a revenue budget, but the determination of all economic policy. (M2)

A second category of reforms aims at the improvement of the revenue budget itself and its presentation. By allowing more public debate on budgetary measures through the use of such parliamentary devices as White Papers, reformers hope to give the public a greater say in what actually appears in the budget. (D1) Furthermore, by the use of more explanatory material, it is hoped to remedy the rather significant problem of comprehension. The highly complex nature of many of the tax measures included in the budget makes it practically unfathomable to all but a few informed experts. (D1)

Finally, reformers have examined the passage of tax legislation through Parliament. The unique parliamentary rules that apply to the budget cause

---

[1] See, for example, Tax Legislative Process Committee, "The Tax Legislative Process" (March-April 1978), 26 *Canadian Tax Journal* 157-81.

[2] As, for example, the Lambert Commission. Canada, Royal Commission on Financial Management and Accountability, *Final Report* (Ottawa: Supply and Services, March 1979).

D1   I agree.

O1   The notion, implicit here, that all personal tax changes could be made
public beforehand without opening up the possibility of using the information
for financial gain is incorrect.

many critics to fear that Parliament has little or no role of substance in the process. Most of the critics focus on the use of Committees of the Whole House, claiming that this precludes any real investigation of the legislation. They advocate a larger role for Standing Committees in the passage of the budget. (D1)

It should be pointed out that not all proposals lend themselves to the categorization used here, of pre-budget, budget, and post-budget reform. Some could equally well be placed in categories other than the ones to which they are assigned in the discussion that follows.

Pre-budget Reform

Critics of the development stage of the budgetary process primarily attack the traditional concept of budget secrecy. By suggesting changes in the ways the Department receives some of its information and by promoting more open forums for the discussion of policy changes, they hope to be able to increase the accountability of the government on financial and economic matters and to reduce the number of tax changes that subsequently have to be amended because of unforeseen difficulties.

Perhaps the most common cry among experts unhappy with the current system is to "open up" the process. The strict rule of budget secrecy that developed when the budget was primarily concerned with raising revenue appears unnecessary for most if not all budget measures today. Although many of the suggestions for reform are extremely vague and ask merely for more openness, there have been some concrete proposals. Perhaps the most straightforward proposal is to define more precisely and hence more narrowly those matters where secrecy is required.

A study for the Carter Commission in 1964 examined the validity of the secrecy rule for the four main areas of taxation: sales or excise taxes, corporate taxes, personal income taxes, and estate taxes.[3] It was found that, in at least the latter two cases, proposed tax changes could be made public beforehand. (O1) At present, the rule of budget secrecy is both unwritten and unqualified. The punishment for a breach of secrecy—resignation—is so severe that ministers are wary indeed about discussing any changes before the budget is tabled. For this reason, former Finance Minister Donald Macdonald, in his budget speech on May 25, 1976, asked that the obligation for secrecy be clarified.[4] Unless the Minister of Finance knows what he can or cannot discuss, he will remain unwilling to divulge any information on budgetary matters.

---

[3] Robert J. Bertrand, Alice Desjardins, and René Hurtubise, *Legislation, Administration and Interpretation Processes in Federal Taxation,* Study for the Royal Commission on Taxation #22 (Ottawa: Queen's Printer, 1967), 46-49.

[4] The Honourable Donald Macdonald, Minister of Finance, *Budget Speech*, May 25, 1976, 25.

M1 All of whom took the oath of secrecy.

D1 This was overplayed. He was within his rights, but he made serious mistakes, was very arrogant in his speech, and antagonized officials and members alike. Also "the three" took an oath of secrecy!

M4 This is what was done in life insurance taxation; the opposition still complained.

M3 There are certain problems: 1) pre-emptive action of private sector to protect themselves from departmental policy; 2) could destroy the psychological leverage of the Minister.

D2 Why doesn't the Tax Foundation or Tax Executives Institute do this as a matter of course, just like C. D. Howe Institute for Policy Analysis does for economic (fiscal) policy? Any private group could make proposals, with rationale.

Although there is a consensus that the process should be opened up to some extent, exactly how, or at what point, this is to be achieved is not always clear. Remembering the Gordon incident in 1963, in which then Finance Minister Walter Gordon was severely criticized for bringing in three outside advisers to aid in writing the budget, (M1, D1) the 1977 report of the Canadian Tax Foundation recommended that the Minister of Finance be allowed to consult private professionals.[5] Although the report preferred the use of more public forums, it suggested that on issues in which secrecy was essential, the Minister should be allowed to retain consultants. These persons would be expected to take an oath of secrecy. (M4)

The CTF report also recommended that for situations in which time or other circumstances do not allow more open consultation, the Minister should be allowed to announce that he has certain options under consideration. This announcement should be made in the House of Commons and should include an invitation to interested parties to provide their views on the issue.

For most budget measures, however, critics believe that secrecy needs to be the exception rather than the rule. The most common recommendation is to set up an investigatory and advisory body. Though the proposals vary as to the appropriate composition and specific functions of such a body, its primary purpose would be to provide a public forum for debate on financial matters. The assumption is that, if all the available options for action were made public, tacit pressure could be placed on the government to justify the choices it makes and that this would result in more informed choices.   (M3, D2)

Appointed Committees

The Carter Commission study referred to previously recommended that a permanent committee composed of civil servants be set up.[6] This committee, called the Tax Advisory Committee, would be responsible for hearing and examining submissions from the public on tax legislation, and sending a report to the Minister of Finance. *"Subject to the Minister's consent,* its reports could be published [my emphasis] ." The study considered a suggestion that 50 per cent of this Committee be drawn from outside the civil service, but felt that the public would rather be heard by the government. As well, the authors were wary about giving a small group of outsiders a disproportionate and unwarranted influence. There are at least two weaknesses in this proposal: first, there is no requirement that the Committee receive submissions publicly; and second, the Minister could decide to suppress the Committee's recommendations. Consequently, aside from the hiring of additional technically qualified civil servants, there would be little change from the existing system.

---

[5] Supra footnote 1, at 171.

[6] Supra footnote 3, at 41.

D2   There could be a Review Board, rather like the Tariff Board—receiving references on structural and technical issues from the Minister.

D2   A complete misunderstanding of the post hoc nature of the Auditor General.

D2   Would this include rates of tax, incentives, tax expenditures, etc.—all policy matters? What would be their criteria—stabilization needs, neutrality, equity, etc.?

D1   I would favour a small, expert, full-time Tax Review Board, probably short-term appointees, a lawyer (even a judge), an accountant or two or an expert tax economist, studying issues referred to them by the Minister, or by an outside organization or taxpayers which the Board considers to merit its attention. It should hold public hearings, in which the members would both question and express criticism—and report publicly to the Minister. It might resemble the Tariff Board in its advisory role. It should *not* get into macroeconomics.

M3   Agreed.

O1   The fact that the forum proposed [in] *Agenda for Cooperation* was multipartite. . .was one of the reasons labour was reluctant to participate in the forum —the other being, of course, the government's unwillingness to terminate controls in the summer of 1977 without an agreement with labour on wage restraint. The lack of such an agreement led to a continuation of controls, and no consultative forum was established.

M4   Indeed, who speaks for businesses or unions that are not specifically recommended? The representative role was always disavowed by businessmen, while the union spokesmen pretended to speak for the whole workforce, organized or not.

D2   The multipartite consultative forum was put forward in response to the Canadian Labour Congress proposal for a tripartite body (government-business-labour) with decision-making powers, including a power to direct investment. The government proposal was to ensure representation from groups other than government-business-labour, and to make clear it was consultative only.

D1   It includes the provinces' information and views.

D2   Because the fiscal projections are based on a joint study with provinces and involve their consent.

O1   In fact, this question is currently being considered. The mid-year report on the fiscal and economic situation could be declassified in the near future. This mid-year report incorporates the effects of the spring round of budgets. In contrast, the January report is on a pre-budget basis and is used by federal and provincial governments in preparing their own budgets. Because of its role as an input in the budget process, it is thought that it should retain its confidential status.

Douglas Sherbaniuk has also recommended the formation of a similar kind of independent Tax Review Board (D2) that would work in conjunction with a parliamentary committee (the latter is discussed below).[7] This Board would function in a manner similar to the Office of the Auditor General. (D2) It would review the tax system, show the options that are open to the government, and recommend changes to particular taxes. (D2) Unlike the former proposals, all the recommendations of this Board would be made public. Presumably, this body would consider both technical and policy matters. If not, the distinction between the two would be most difficult to draw in practice.

(D1)

The proposals described so far involved setting up bodies solely for the purpose of examining tax legislation. The Liberal government, in contrast, recommended forming a multipartite forum for discussions of overall economic policy. In *Agenda for Cooperation*, it was suggested that a body be created, made up of 30 to 50 people drawn from all sectors of society, and chaired by the federal government.[8] It would analyse information from a wide variety of sources, including the government, and in so doing help "lead to a better common understanding of the realities of the economic situation and the limits within which the economy is evolving."[9] This body would have no decision-making powers and would not be expected to produce any final conclusions. The forum would be influential only insofar as increased public input on, and better public knowledge of, economic affairs would affect the actual policy makers. In my opinion, these tripartite forums are difficult to reconcile with a parliamentary form of government. (M3, O1) Who speaks for those who are neither businessmen nor union members? (M4, D2) Generally, such bodies produce much rhetoric and little agreement except on proposals that would be detrimental to the interests not represented. Certainly, the protagonists do not need an additional forum in which to express their demands.

The *Agenda* also suggested that the analyses and projections given by the Minister of Finance at the Federal-Provincial Meeting of Finance Ministers and Provincial Treasurers be made available to this committee and that this information also be tabled in the House of Commons.[10] The question arises, "Why isn't this being done with or without such a forum? " (D1, D2, O1)

The primary advantage of an appointed body is that it may be composed of people who are already competent and well informed on financial and/or taxation matters. It would be capable of dealing with complicated issues and, at least in the case of the latter proposal, provide technical advice tempered

---

[7]Douglas Sherbaniuk, "Budget Secrecy" (May-June 1976), 24 *Canadian Tax Journal* 223-30, at 227.

[8]Canada, Anti-inflation Board, *Agenda for Cooperation (1977): A Discussion Paper on Decontrol and Post-Control Issues* (Ottawa: Supply and Services, 1977), 28-33.

[9]Ibid., 32.

[10]Ibid.

D2   That is, a political judgment.

D2   Or even irresponsibly.

D2   I think this would make sense on certain kinds of questions—for example, as referred by the Minister, like a Tariff Board reference—with or without an "issues" paper submitted by the Minister.

O1   The process of scrutiny by a [parliamentary] committee was followed for the report of the Commodity Tax Review Group, though hearings were not completed because of the Committee's work on the Bank Act.

D1   The Auditor General operates after the fact, not before.

D2   No—quite a different function.

D2   Impossible, unless we change parliamentary government to [a] congressional system as in [the] United States.

D2   Not fiscal policy.

by a sensitivity to public opinion. (D2) The fact that it would have no decision-making responsibilities might also be an advantage, in that it would be
able to deal with a wider range of issues, more freely. (D2) Critics have, however, seen some problems with this sort of institution. A number of critics
have suggested giving similar responsibilities to parliamentary committees,
bodies that do have a right to claim to "speak for the people." But such committees are not without their limitations either.

Parliamentary Committees

In addition to an independent tax board, Douglas Sherbaniuk recommended
that either a new parliamentary committee be created or that the mandate of
the House of Commons Standing Committee on Finance, Trade and Economic
Affairs be extended to study proposals for tax changes. (D2) This committee
would hear testimony from the government, tax professionals and the general
public, and make a recommendation about any proposal being made. (O1)
Sherbaniuk suggested that the work of this committee could be combined
with that of the independent agency in a manner similar to the relationship
between the Public Accounts Committee and the Auditor General's Office.[11]
(D1, D2)

The CTF report expanded upon this proposal. It recommended the formation of a taxation subcommittee of the Standing Committee on Finance, Trade
and Economic Affairs.[12] The subcommittee would study all major tax policy
changes, perhaps through issuance of a White, Green, or Brown Paper, before
they became law.[13] In addition, the report recommended that the Minister
of Finance be allowed to refer proposals for fiscal policy or structural changes
to the subcommittee for discussion before the budget was drafted. (D2) It
was felt that he would welcome the additional input on such far-reaching decisions as are present in a budget. Increased study of structural changes would
allow an opportunity to discover weaknesses that may have escaped the Department of Finance. Recognizing the need for some budget secrecy, the report left it up to the Minister to decide which proposals would be discussed.
(D2) It was also recommended that the subcommittee have a role to play in
the passage of the budget through Parliament. (This recommendation will be
examined in more detail later.) It is difficult to know how much use the Minister would actually make of such a body. It is possible that, unless he were
forced to use it, he would ignore it. Although the report recommended that
the subcommittee be adequately staffed, access to information almost certainly would pose a problem. The report agreed that testimony from Finance

---

[11] Supra footnote 7, at 227.

[12] Supra footnote 1, at 177.

[13] Ibid., at 166.

D2   In some ways, this is a transfer from [the] U.S. congressional system, with its Joint Economic Committee, hearings, and reports. Is it appropriate to the parliamentary system? Is the Committee to operate on party lines? Is the government (Minister) bound by it? If [the Minister] rejects the proposals, how do the government members subsequently vote in the Commons? Where does the Bank fit in? Are other ministers responsible for structural policies?

M3   Improve the Department of Finance and forget about more committees.

D2   Of course not. Will it have its own expert staff? Does it hold the budget hearings whenever the government decides on a budget—in November as well as in the spring? Can the Minister take any kind of fiscal or tax policy action without waiting for the Committee?

O2   Crosbie budget.

M4   A new committee is not needed. The Finance Committee could well hold hearings early in the year, giving an opportunity to outsiders, deemed to be qualified, to express their views, and hearing from the Minister on his pre-budget perspectives of the economy. It need not make a report—probably should not because of the want of confidence question when the budget comes down.

The tax bills could well be placed before the Committee. The only reason for not dispensing with the Committee of the Whole was that in December 1968 so many radical changes were being made in the legislature procedure, it was felt that the budget should be allowed to remain in the House.

M4   See earlier skepticism about long-term projections.

D2   What is the purpose of the budget debate?

D2   Has this improved economic policy making in the United Kingdom or the United States?

officials could be treated as confidential, as could the advice given by officials to the Minister, and it claimed that such difficulties would be exceptions. The past conduct of the Department, however, suggests otherwise.

A study for the Business Council on National Issues (BCNI) put forward a similar proposal.[14] The authors agreed that taxation policy should be reviewed in a subcommittee of the Standing Committee on Finance, Trade and Economic Affairs. Instead of making this subcommittee responsible for studying fiscal policy also, though, they recommended the formation of a Joint House of Commons-Senate Committee to examine all areas of economic policy. This body would hold pre-budget hearings and provide a forum for public scrutiny of annual reviews issued by the Economic Council of Canada (ECC). It would examine these reviews and hear testimony from government ministers and officials, in addition to nongovernmental sources, and then provide evaluations of, and recommendations for, overall economic policy. (D2) The hearings of this Committee would be televised.[15] The only advantage that this proposal has over the previous one is the fact that the workload would be shared among two committees rather than one. There seems to be no particular advantage in restricting the second body to scrutiny of the ECC reports. (M3, D2)

The BCNI study also recommended the establishment of a formal fiscal planning process. The Minister of Finance and the President of the Treasury Board would be required to publish annually a paper that would *project*, from three to five years in advance, government expenditures and revenues. (O2) It would also include a medium-term economic *forecast* and the assumptions lying behind it. This plan would be updated and presented to Parliament annually. The authors recommended that another new Standing Committee be established to review the plan. (M4) The publication of this "fiscal framework" would provide both knowledge about the government's view of the economy and an opportunity to debate this view.[16]

A similar recommendation was also made in a paper by Gail Cook.[17] Cook argued that the government's fiscal framework should be exposed to parliamentary debate and that it should include "the implications of current policy and expenditure commitments over the ensuing five years."[18] (M4, D2) She also suggested that a parliamentary committee study the report and then draw up its own economic framework. She pointed out that such a plan had operated in both Great Britain and the United States. (D2)

---

[14]Thomas d'Aquino, G. Bruce Doern, and Cassandra Blair, *Parliamentary Government in Canada: A Critical Assessment and Suggestions for Change,* a study for the Business Council on National Issues (Ottawa: Intercounsel Limited, 1979), 77.

[15]Ibid., 77-78.

[16]Ibid., 72.

[17]Gail Cook, *Economic Decision-Making: A Structural Problem* (Montreal: C. D. Howe Research Institute, October 1977).

[18]Ibid., 19.

D2　I think there is incredible naiveté in most of this. There is complete confusion between fiscal projections on the basis of established and immediately proposed (in the budget) spending and taxing on the one hand, and a multiyear plan involving proposed changes in policy, both taxing and spending, year by year. Even just the former is incredibly difficult, given all the uncertainties and a spelling out of economic assumptions, and we can scarcely forecast cyclical changes. And how can one aspire to the latter? How does it fit into the lifespan of a government? We know the aberrations of Soviet planning. How does the government telegraph whatever nebulous thoughts it may have on policy change in advance, and take account of feedback effects? The only way to go, in my view, is a target exercise of the kind the Department prepared for the first ministers conference of 1978, or the quantitative projections based on "no policy change."

D1　Not necessarily explicit.

D1　Hold hearings on it—summon witnesses.

D1　That is really too much—but the tax bills should probably go there if the Lambert Commission proposals [are] accepted.

D2　Try forecasting the actual (not trend) movement [of] the economy quarterly up to 1985—including all the fiscal program changes by governments including the provinces, and the appropriate federal fiscal responses each year or quarter. What does the plan include for energy prices, the Fiscal Arrangements Act of 1982-87, Canada Pension Plan or unemployment insurance changes, etc., etc.?

M3　Agreed.

Perhaps the most extensive proposal for a "fiscal plan" is that recommended by the Lambert Commission.[19] The Commission proposed that a small
secretariat within the Department of Finance, in co-operation with the PCO
and the TBS, initiate the development of the plan. The final plan would:

1) set government priorities and its means of achieving them;

2) evaluate the government's past performance;

3) analyse the balance between revenues and expenditures; and

4) evaluate all proposed programs with regard to their impact on the plan.
(D2)

The plan would be presented—with the prior approval of the Prime Minister
(D1)—to the Cabinet Committee on Priorities and Planning and then be distributed to the heads of the departments. The plan would be tabled in October
and automatically be referred to a new Standing Committee of the House of
Commons. The Committee would then make a report by a fixed deadline, and
the report would provide the basis for a two-day debate. (D1) Responsibilities
of the Committee would also include examining how all legislation—in particular, the budget—would affect the plan and presumably recommending for or
against any deviations from the framework.[20] (D1)

Obviously, the concept of an extended and published fiscal framework has
ramifications that would extend far beyond the production of a budget. By
exposing the government's economic policies to public scrutiny and debate
and by requiring it to justify any changes in those policies, the fiscal plan could
increase the overall accountability of the government, and particularly of the
Department of Finance. The budget would have to be produced with an eye
to maintaining consistency with the fiscal plan or rationalizing deviation from
it or revisions in it. As a result, many of its broad effects might be easily pre-
dicted in advance. This increase of information from the government could
well increase the amount of influence of those not directly involved in the current process of economic policy making. Everything would be a great deal
more explicit.

The five-year fiscal plan concept, however, has a number of problems. (D2)
There are inherent dangers, in the first place, in making "assumptions" about
economic situations. When government forecasts can influence behaviour, to
provide the assumption, is, in effect, to generate anticipatory moves that may
be perverse. As well, assumptions that may depend on a number of variables
may produce innumerable plans. Do innumerable priorities also have to be
presented? The political difficulties are great as well. Can ministers be bound
to a three-to-five-year plan?[21] (M3)

---

[19] Supra footnote 2, at 71-91.

[20] Ibid., 381-83.

[21] I have discussed these problems in a previous paper. See Douglas G. Hartle, "The
Report of the Royal Commission on Financial Management and Accountability (The
Lambert Report): A Review" (Summer 1979), 5 *Canadian Public Policy* 366-82.

D2   Projections only—not a five-year plan.

M4   In the light of interest rate changes, how meaningful are those forecasts only five months later? And where will they be in 25 months?

D1   They disregarded this material. It was too difficult for them.

D2   They were scarcely noted by the media, which always complains about lack of information, and then about being unable to read or understand the amount that is produced.

M3   Agreed.

M4   Despite all their rhetoric, did they actually set up a committee study on anything?

D1   Adversarial party system.

M4   Exactly. The Lambert Commission failed to recognize that a committee is the microcosm of the House. Government is carried on by partisan contest, and government members will not shoot the puck in their own net, nor the opposition in theirs. If the Lambert Commission really wanted independence and power for the committee and this occurred, you would have stalemate, not smoother operation of the system.

D2   The major problem (in the Commons committee Finance, Trade and Economic Affairs) is to reduce its adversarial approach. It is almost always used as a forum by the opposition to try to discredit the government except when it is working on specific legislation, when it can do first-rate work.

The Crosbie budget speech did, of course, go some distance toward implementing the concept of a five-year fiscal plan. It contained five-year projections of budgetary revenues and expenditures (D2) (and therefore of the deficit) *and* forecasts of inflation and unemployment rates. It is understood that it was the intention of the Clark administration to release projections of the nine expenditure envelopes. As was stated earlier, a bill was introduced, which died on the Order Paper, to strengthen parliamentary committees—although not as substantially as Lambert had recommended. Although the information provided in the budget was certainly used to great effect against the Clark government in the ensuing election campaign, few would argue that it was the basis for the defeat of the government in the budget vote or of the defeat of that administration in the ensuing election. The effects (if any) on private expectations of revealing the government's pessimistic forecasts will never be known, because of the uncertainty created by the almost immediate defeat of the government. For all that, one has the impression that the projections and forecasts per se were well received by the media and presumably by the electorate. (M4, D1, D2) Furthermore, one might speculate that it will be extremely difficult for subsequent administrations to deny this kind of information, however apprehensive they might be about the consequences.

Those critics who have recommended increased use of parliamentary committees have recognized that often these committees have been ineffective in the past. Proposals have also been made, therefore, to increase the power of these committees. In particular, the Lambert Report addressed itself to the problem. The Commission recommended:

1) restructuring of the old committee system to make it more streamlined and efficient;

2) restrictions on the use of substitutions of members to the committee;

3) election of committee chairmen for the life of the Parliament and appropriate remuneration for that responsibility; and

4) provision of staff for the committees.[22] (M3)

The intention was to increase the prestige of the committees and to allow them to play a more effective role in government. Certainly, any attempt to increase the effectiveness of these committees would be welcome in most quarters—the government of the day presumably being the exception, and the Clark administration being the exception to the exception! (M4) But there are inherent difficulties. (D1) How could strict party discipline be circumvented? (M4, D2) What could be done with the reports of such committees?

Most of the "pre-budget" recommendations for reform are not meant to fit directly into the budgetary process. Instead, by providing a public forum—through either an independent agency or a parliamentary committee—to dis-

---

[22]Supra footnote 2, at 585, recommendations 22.1, 22.2, 22.3, 22.4.

M4   Agreed.

D2   What are election and campaign promises all about?

M3   Is this consistent with parliamentary goals?

M3   Pre-emptive action would be taken by [the] private sector.

M3   Agreed.

D2   After receiving the voluminous Carter Commission report initiated in 1963 and submitted in 1968.

cuss taxation policy and/or other economic policies, they would offer an opportunity for better informing the general public about the issues involved. (M4) Open presentations to these institutions would afford an opportunity for interested parties to exchange views and debate issues. With the publication of the options open to government, there would be increased pressure on the government to justify the choices that were made. The use of a fiscal plan would increase the accountability of government for overall economic policy. If the government were forced to express its views and future intentions, (D2) informed criticism would be facilitated: the issues would be clarified and the opportunities for discussion expanded.

The proposals for reform described so far aim at changing the procedure before the fact, so to speak. By increasing public knowledge of taxation and economic issues, reformers seek to give the public a greater say in the determination of government policy. (M3) The following two sections examine proposals for the treatment of tax structure changes both tentative and actual.

Changes in Budget Content and Presentation

A number of proposals have been made dealing with the way the budget is presented in Parliament. These reforms usually have one of two main purposes. First, it is argued that putting forward tentative budgetary measures for debate (M3) could achieve increased parliamentary or public participation in the process. Second, the inclusion of explanatory material with the budget would help ensure better public understanding of the government's actions. (M3)

The recommendation that more use be made of government papers of one colour or another has already been mentioned. The purpose of a White Paper is to express the government's view on proposed policy issues and to invite interested parties to voice their opinions. It is hoped that out of this discussion can come more informed and politically sensitive legislation. The most popular example of the method's benefits is its use in the development of the Tax Reform Bill of 1971.[23] In late 1969, the federal government tabled a document that outlined the proposals of the government for reforming the tax system. (D2) The paper was referred to two parliamentary committees—the House Standing Committee on Finance, Trade and Economic Affairs and the Senate Standing Committee on Banking, Trade and Commerce—which were asked to examine it, hold public hearings, and then make their recommendations. Following a year of extensive participation from both the Department of Finance and the public, the committees presented their reports for the government's consideration, and the ultimate reforms were enacted in the budget of June 1971.[24]

---

[23] Audrey Doerr, " The Role of White Papers," in G. Bruce Doern and Peter Aucoin, eds., *The Structures of Policy-Making in Canada* (Toronto: Macmillan, 1971), 179-203, at 184-87.

[24] Ibid., at 187-97.

M3   This is now done with sales tax, GATT, etc.

M4   I always doubted that the 1969-1971 exercise was worth the trauma.

D1   One will have to avoid overloading the parliamentary committees—hence the need for a Tax Review Committee.

M4   Nobody pretends the Excise Tax Act is wonderful, but this technique of policy paper discussion was used with respect to commodity taxes and has resulted in no change. The fact [is] that a White Paper is attacked by vested interests, and a government which has said it wants to hear all viewpoints cannot respond to the most virulent and partisan attacks because then it loses its objectivity.

D2   We tried this also with the Green or White Papers on the sales tax. The resulting lack of interest, except from those opposed to its main thrust, was to set back reform in this area indefinitely! The impartial tax experts who complain about lack of participation never turned up.

D2   The time factor is well illustrated in the Bank Act. After six years' work and four bills and three extensions, we may now see the new Act.

M3   Agreed.

D2   This can happen even in a final budget proposal: taxation of life insurance proceeds in order to get at main investment and income component was just shot down.

M3   Governments have to take a stand with an open door policy. This is unnecessary.

D2   No more than. . .Lambert's final plan.

While this example dealt only with tax reform, some experts believe that the White Paper process could be used for examination of proposals for specific tax changes. Douglas Sherbaniuk, the CTF study referred to earlier, and a former deputy recommended greater use of this method.[25] They would have the Minister of Finance refer White Papers proposing structure changes to the House Standing Committee on Finance, Trade and Economic Affairs (or a subcommittee thereof) before the changes were incorporated into the budget. (M3) By allowing debate before a proposal went into a budget, it would be possible to discover and remedy both technical and political weaknesses in the legislation. (M4) This particular method would give Parliament and particularly its Standing Committees (D1) a greater role in the budgetary process.

(M4, D2)

The merits of this proposal—that it encourages greater public input, that it gives Parliament a role in the budgetary process, that it may allow the Standing Committees an opportunity to be more effective—may not outweigh its disadvantages. The greatest problem seems to be the time factor. The White Paper on Tax Reform took over a year to be considered and there were still complaints that not all views were heard. How much time would be allowed these committees to consider the papers? (D2) How much interest could be generated among parliamentarians and the public to examine them? There may also be procedural problems with the use of Standing Committees. (These are examined in the last section.) From the government's point of view, White Papers can create added political problems by providing an opportunity for well-organized special-interest groups to marshall campaigns, while the more general interest is, by and large, leashed. (M3, D2)

The Honourable E. J. Benson, the former Finance Minister who certainly had experience with the use of White Papers, carried the suggestion yet further. In an address to an estate tax conference in 1969, he recommended that the tradition that a government stand or fall on the success of its budget be re-examined.[26] Instead, he suggested, a tentative budget should be presented to the House for discussion, and the government should be allowed to make modifications following that debate. In this way, he believed, the Minister could get a much-needed outside reaction to his proposals, without risk of defeat.[27] (M3) This proposal seems idealistic enough to be attractive and impractical enough to be rejected. (D2) What government would be willing to retract what it has already stated to be its views on the budget? True, something of the sort did happen in 1963, but "willing" hardly seems the appropriate adjective to describe that government's actions.

---

[25] Supra footnote 7, at 227; supra footnote 1, at 166; and information obtained in interviews.

[26] Supra footnote 23, at 185.

[27] *The Globe and Mail,* March 20, 1969. Also quoted in supra footnote 7, at 224, and supra footnote 1, at 161, n. 16.

D2   CCH does this very well.

D2   We would certainly need more staff and would have to upgrade salaries considerably to get and hold the people required. The government can't compete with the gravy in the private sector in the tax area. The general public is rarely interested, but I can understand[that] the tax practitioners (CTF members) who make their living at this would like help.

O1   Recent practice has included presenting draft legislation in the form of an amended ways and means motion in advance of tabling the final motion and bill. This has been done to allow interested parties to make suggestions for changes.

D1   Why? Surely the recent trend is to issue numerous advance papers on special problems.

D2   I do not think this was ever a main consideration—but lack of time and staff services raises a major problem. [One] of the main purposes of the press briefing on the budget was to provide just such explanations.

O1   With regard to the utilization of outside technical advice, it is worth noting that for the past few years the Department has had tax practitioners from the private sector on staff for one-year appointments in order to provide such advice.

M4   This is a division not easy to make in practice.

In addition to procedural changes, reformers have pointed to a need for changes in the budget itself. Douglas Sherbaniuk, the BCNI study, and the CTF report all recommended that more explanatory material accompany the presentation of the budget papers.[28] The increasingly complicated technical material in the budget and growing numbers of amendments and re-amendments require an immense investment of time and effort simply to understand what exactly is being done. A memorandum that described how the new changes would affect the status quo, and explained *why* the changes were made, would go a long way in reducing the cost to the public of understanding the budget. (D2) While such a proposal has been resisted because of a lack of time to prepare such a paper during the budget "gestation" stage, the CTF study claimed the matter was so vital that the Department should expand its staff, or else bring in private consultants, (D2) for the express purpose of writing the memorandum.[29] This device would not only increase the public understanding of the government's action; by forcing the government to justify these actions, the accountability of the government to the public also may be increased. (O1)

One suspects that one reason the Department has not provided more explanatory material is that it often does not wish to admit publicly what it is trying to do with particular tax measures. (D1, D2) The step beyond a few vague lines in a speech may be not a memorandum but a book. By the same token, because proposals are developed internally, some quickly and without the aid of outside technical advice, officials may not wish to reveal the uncertainties in their minds with respect to all of the technical implications. (O1) Here, too, a thorough explanation of how the measure would work could often involve a long complex statement and, in the eyes of officials, simply give aid and comfort to those who seek to raid the public purse.

Post-budget Reform

The CTF study recommended that consideration be given to changing the (budget) procedure after the budget debate.[30] It proposed that the budget actually be divided into two bills, or be considered as a split bill, in order to differentiate between what the study described as structural changes and policy changes. Policy changes are either tax policy measures—the decision to implement a new tax or drastically alter an old one—or fiscal, social, or economic measures. (M4) As was mentioned above, the study recommended extensive debate on policy issues before they were implemented, suggesting that a subcommittee of the House Standing Committee on Finance, Trade and Economic Affairs might be a suitable forum. The authors of the report still felt,

---

[28] Supra footnote 7, at 228-29; supra footnote 14, at 65; supra footnote 1, at 173.

[29] Supra footnote 1, at 173-74.

[30] Ibid., at 163-64, 174.

D2   I think there is considerable merit in most of these proposals.

M4   See earlier comments about the committee system. It seems to me that a system which says nothing is definite until Royal Assent creates far more uncertainty than one which says the proposal is effective *now* unless a specific change is made.

however, that fiscal and equity considerations required that such changes, once decided upon, usually should go into effect immediately on budget night. (D2)

On the other hand, structural changes—"amendments related to the machinery or structure of the tax system"[31]—need not be in force until after Royal Assent. The CTF report recommended that, rather than considering all budgetary measures in a Committee of the Whole House after second reading, structural changes should be sent to a House Standing Committee for consideration (M4)—once again, perhaps the Standing Committee on Finance, Trade and Economic Affairs. There, witnesses from both the Department of Finance and the interested public could be heard on the merits of the bill. While changes could not be made in the general purpose of the legislation, amendments that would make the bill more effective could be more readily achieved. In addition, testimony from Finance officials would further public understanding of the objectives of the particular measure.[32]

There is a significant difference between the two-bill and the split-bill approach. The former involves presenting two bills to the House following the budget.[33] The onus presumably would be on the Minister of Finance to determine which of his measures would be in the "structural" or the "policy" bills. The split-bill approach (which has been used in Great Britain) involves presenting a single bill to Parliament. Parliament then decides whether or not to refer more complicated provisions to a Standing Committee. Since the passage of the bill as a whole cannot take place until these provisions have been reported upon, the Committee is under some pressure to act quickly.[34] The CTF study did not recommend one alternative over the other.

The report did not discount the problems inherent in separating policy changes from structural changes, but it claimed that it would not matter if some structural changes that also had policy overtones were sent to a committee. The problem comes in deciding when the measure is to take effect. If it is to take effect immediately, then it seems to be automatically a policy change (although this is not always the case). It seems that no matter which of the above options (bills) were chosen, because the Minister would be the one to choose when measures were to take effect, he would determine which were structural and which were policy changes. And because the Minister already has the authority to choose when measures are effective, there would be no great change. In the budgets of April 10 and November 16, 1978, measures were made effective on Royal Assent. One wonders whether the CTF proposal would ensure that this would occur more frequently.

---

[31] Ibid., at 165.

[32] Ibid., at 174.

[33] Ibid.

[34] Ibid., at 175-76.

M3   The committee of whole House is a better forum except for a few narrow technical matters.

D2   These could be adapted to assist the objective. They are as man-made as budget secrecy.

D1   Yes.

M4   The procedure now provides for an overall time limit at the report stage; it should also provide for such a time limit at the committee stage.

A3   This would confer on ways and means processes the functions performed before 1968 by Supply Committee!

M3   Agreed.

O1   Sherbaniuk's suggestion. . .is worth consideration. However, it must be recognized that it would not be desirable for the House to have before it at any one time more than one bill amending the same Act. This would just lead to confusion and would stand in the way of proper consideration of the bills in question.

D2   Very much so.

Standing Committees are not now used for taxation matters because of procedural rules: (M3, D2)

1) A motion to refer various clauses in the budget (assuming a split-bill report) to a Standing Committee is debatable. What if such motions were made on each separate clause causing the resultant debate? Indeed, it would be in the interest of the opposition to refer all matters to the Standing Committee for scrutiny.

2) Closure cannot be invoked in a Standing Committee, unlike a Committee of the Whole House. It is conceivable that a tax bill would be held up indefinitely in the Committee.[35] Perhaps, as Lambert suggests with the consideration of the fiscal plan, the Committee could be required to meet a specific deadline. (D1) Deadlines do not seem to affect procedure in the United Kingdom.

3) Amendments cannot be moved on reports of Committees of the Whole House. This is not the case with reports of Standing Committees. Innumerable amendments might be moved, and closure would have to be invoked on each amendment.[36] (M4)

The recommendation of the Lambert Report that reports from Committees should not have to be debated might be a partial solution. But if the reports are not debated, what purpose do they serve? Time is the main problem with this proposal. It might well take many weeks for a Committee to consider a tax bill, even if there were no attempt to stall. If there were stalling, the bill might never get passed. The opposition would be given a potentially very powerful tool. Time may not be of so much importance for structural changes, but surely it is still a factor.[37]   (A3)

Another alternative was suggested by Douglas Sherbaniuk. Since 1968, the Standing Orders of the House of Commons have allowed ways and means motions to be tabled without a budget.[38] Sherbaniuk recommended that more complicated changes be made outside the budget. This option would help make the budget itself somewhat less of a ponderous and unfathomable document. It would also allow more time for examination of these other proposals.[39] (M3)   (O1)

Presumably, Sherbaniuk primarily means structural changes: but tax policy changes could conceivably be included as well. Is a "provision relating to corporate reorganization" a structural change or a tax policy change? The distinction may be in the eye of the beholder. (D2)

---

[35] John Stewart, "The Tax Reform Bill in Parliament" (January-February 1971), 19 *Canadian Tax Journal* 1-7, at 5.

[36] Ibid.

[37] D'Aquino, Doern, and Blair make a recommendation similar to that of the CTF. Supra footnote 14.

[38] Supra footnote 35, at 3-4.

[39] Supra footnote 7, at 228.

D2   I come back again to the point that it can't be a *plan*. It can be a projection of costs of existing programs and yields of existing tax structure, all based upon assumptions or trend forecasts of the economy, continuously updated; *or* it can be a more generalized target exercise, in which economic and fiscal objectives are consistent and as realistic as possible.

M3   Nice and tidy, but is life really like this? Many proposals intend in effect to substitute other sources of advice for that of the Deputy of Finance. Surely this could be met practically by strengthening the Department and giving it more authority over other departments on economic matters. Collegial government is weakening the cabinet structure and the accountability of individual ministers and departments. A more open Department and a more accessible Minister would meet many of the criticisms.

D2   I think the whole discussion has to be set against the background of the operation of the parliamentary system of responsible government, and the role of parties in that system. A great deal can be done to improve technical discussion, but the thrust of economic policy is surely a political matter, for which the government is accountable to Parliament and ultimately the electorate. I tend to think the retention of the Liberal government in power is partly due to a general acceptance of its economic policies and the performance of the economy, even up to the most recent times. If we can get away from the enforced resignation of the Minister, the so-called "budget" leaks, we can go far [toward] reducing the secondary problem—but not until then. Even in my short period, there was scarcely a budget where that issue was not raised to the discomfort of the Minister and myself. I also think there is merit in the *"multipartite" consultative* forum—if all participants besides the government accept a feedback role to their respective constituencies. If it were composed of people of ability who [were] prepared to serve as objectively as possible, it could function much like the U.S. Joint Economic Committee. But again it would be a 24-hour media event, unless it could minimize internal conflicts. Other than that I think the split-bill technique and Standing Committee approach [have] merit, as well as a Review Board (like the Tariff Board) to do special studies on references from the Minister. Such a board could have a permanent nucleus, but be added to, or establish special panels for specific studies—e.g. indexing capital gains, life insurance, taxation of charities or co-operatives. It could hold public meetings and use expert staff. In all this, however, ultimate ministerial responsibility, and hence decision making, [have] to remain as fundamental.

A3   To the concerns you lay out (masterfully, I think) in Chapter 3, most of the Lambert Commission and other proposals are at best irrelevant and at worst pernicious. The proposals are irrelevant to the integration of monetary and fiscal policy and to the dependence of the process on personalities. Opening up the process, especially through meaningful pre- and post-budget parliamentary committee consideration (if such be genuinely possible under our constitution), would have the following pernicious effects:

1) It would create a forum for jurisdictional disputes even more fractious, given the presence of the opposition, than Cabinet.

2) It would create a conduit for pressure for tax expenditures.

3) It would heighten uncertainty, inasmuch as it would delay the imposition and possibly alter the character of tax changes.

These effects would be more likely in minority situations than majority ones. Now there may still be an argument for opening the process up. It might improve the flow of information to both actors and observers, and it might make the process more "representative" and thus possibly more legitimate than it is now. But it would *not*, I believe, remedy most of the problems you identify in Chapter 3, and it would worsen some.

Finally, the fiscal plan envisaged by the Lambert Commission (D2) would require that all tax legislation be referred to the new Standing Committee on Government Finance and the Economy. The Committee would have to examine whether or not the new legislation conformed to the fiscal plan and, if it did not, require the government to justify its deviation.[40] The Committee would then, one might suppose, report its findings to the House. (M3, D2, A3)

---

[40] Supra footnote 2, at 408.

5

Conclusions

The preceding chapters lean primarily on the information obtained from the interviewees, David Good's dissertation,[1] published sources, and the commentators. In order to let this material shine through, I have suppressed my own views except where it seemed necessary for me to fill in gaps or provide continuity. Where I have breached this self-denying ordinance, I have tried to make that fact explicit in the text. This chapter, however, is different. It largely reflects my own perceptions, experience, inferences, and speculations. To the extent that one can have independent opinions not totally coloured by what one has learned from others, this chapter reflects my opinions.

Some Alternative Frameworks of Analysis

It has been my view for several years that collective decision making can best be understood as the outcome of the interplay among four distinct games: the political game, the bureaucratic game, the special-interest-group game, and the media game.[2] The term "game" is used to denote a situation in which the selection of players, the responsibilities assigned to each of the positions they occupy, the object(s) of the game, and the rewards and punishments attached to particular kinds of plays are determined by explicit and inexplicit rules that are unique to each game. There is also a set of rules that prescribes the nature of the play between and among each of the games. The players seek to maximize their own utility—that is to say, they pursue their self-interest—within the context of the rules of the game (incentives and constraints) in which they are engaged. This entails the pursuit of victory in one's own game.

The term "game" is also intended to denote the strategic nature of the play. In order to win, it is necessary not only to "do one's own thing" in splendid isolation, but also to act in anticipation of the actions and reactions of the other players—those on one's own team, in one's own game, and in the other three related games. These moves by other players, who themselves are seeking advancement, cannot be known in advance with certainty. A fuller ac-

---

[1] David A. Good, "The Politics of Anticipation" (Ph.D. dissertation, University of California, Berkeley, 1979).

[2] See Douglas G. Hartle, *Public Policy Decision Making and Regulation* (Montreal: Institute for Research on Public Policy, 1980).

count of this games approach to policy making can be found in an earlier publication of mine and a book by Aaron Wildavsky.[3]

This study was never envisaged as a "test" of the use of the gaming approach as a framework for understanding the revenue budget process. The selection of the interviewees, the questioning, and the draft text would have been quite different had that been my purpose. Indeed, had that been my purpose, it probably would have been more sensible to seek to describe and analyse in depth either a particular budget or, perhaps better still, a particular major tax structure change, such as the introduction of partial indexation of the personal income tax. But it seemed sensible first to undertake this more descriptive and less analytical work as a prior step to these more ambitious investigations. It is not surprising, therefore, that this study provides little, if any, basis for accepting or rejecting the games framework to public policy decision making. It certainly seems, however, to leave two alternative frameworks in some disarray.[4]

The "rational actor model" approach was developed as an integral part of modern welfare economics. It assumes that some all-knowing, all-powerful, undefined entity pursues the maximum realization of *the* goals of society (the so-called social welfare function that encompasses *the* set of weighted objectives of society). This is accomplished through changes in the all-inclusive (infinitely large) set of policy instruments, such as tax levels and structures, expenditure programs, and regulations.[5] This conceptualization of policy determination perhaps has a place in normative theory: from this set of assumptions, one can deduce the conditions that must prevail for this hypothetical optimum to be reached without regard to institutional detail. But it is not intended to be either a description of reality or a useful postulate in a theory designed to predict government behaviour. Nevertheless, probably unconsciously and certainly without rigour, some economists have written or thought as though there were, or should be, some set of generally accepted objectives and as though governments were, or should be, trying to maximize the realization of these objectives for the good of society. The information gathered for this study, by its nature, cannot be used to address the question: should governments have a set of well-defined and weighted objectives? Nor can it be used to address the question: would it be feasible for governments to specify

---

[3] Ibid., 173-96, and Aaron Wildavsky, *The Politics of the Budgetary Process*, 2nd ed. (Boston: Little Brown, 1974).

[4] Heretofore I have thought of the games approach as a framework that is helpful in understanding how decisions are made by a given set of actors competing within a given set of rules that determines the structure and process. This study raises, but does not answer, some questions about the games that are played in order to change those rules.

[5] James M. Buchanan, "The Achievement and the Limits of Public Choice in Diagnosing Government Failure and in Offering Bases for Constructive Reform," an unpublished paper prepared for presentation at the International Symposium "Anatomy of Government Deficiencies," Diessen om Ammersee, Bavaria, July 1980.

such an all-inclusive set of objectives?[6] But the information obtained makes it possible to put together a strong case that those responsible in the recent past for one of the most significant bundles of policy instruments in the Department of Finance did not think they were doing what many economists and public administrators thought they were doing (or at least thought they should be doing). This will come as no surprise to anyone who has had even a remote acquaintance with the real world of collective decision making, public or private.[7]

The descriptions/injunctions of political scientists and public administrators fare no better.[8] According to the formalist school of public administration, officials limit themselves, or should limit themselves, to the provision of technical advice. This takes the form of presentations to ministers of the feasible policy alternatives, together with an objective assessment of their respective pros and cons. Nonspecialist ministers, according to this school, confine themselves to choosing on the basis of their political judgment one policy from among the group of alternatives presented to them. From the interviews carried out for this study, and from the comments received on the draft, it is apparent that the roles of officials and ministers are not narrowly prescribed. Senior Finance officials, in fact, gave political advice to ministers; and some ministers (for example, M3) were involved, in a nontrivial way, in fairly technical matters. There is, then, no neat separation of ministerial and bureaucratic roles.

The Politics of Anticipation

David Good in his dissertation (and in his book derived from it)[9] used an analytic concept derived from Aaron Wildavsky's *The Politics of the Budgetary Process*.[10] (Good's title, "The Politics of Anticipation," is, indeed, the short name for Wildavsky's concept.) The basic idea is that, in both words and actions, men are influenced to a significant extent by the anticipated reactions of others. Thus, subordinates refrain from presenting arguments for or against alternatives when they anticipate that their superiors will reject them out of

---

[6] The difficulties involved in spelling out such objectives are discussed in supra footnote 2, at 173-96.

[7] A realistic appraisal of how decisions are made can be found in Allen Schick, "The Road to PPB: the Stages of Budget Reform" (December 1966), 26 *Public Administration Review* 243-58; "Systems for Analysis: PPB and its Alternatives," in U.S. Congress, Joint Economic Committee, *The Analysis and Evaluation of Public Expenditures: The PPB System*, vol. 3 (Washington, D.C.: U.S. Government Printing Office, 1969), 817-34; and *Congress and Money: Budgetary Spending and Taxing* (Washington, D.C.: The Urban Institute, 1980), 1-60.

[8] Robert MacGregor Dawson, *The Government of Canada*, 5th ed., rev. by Norman Ward (Toronto: University of Toronto Press, 1970).

[9] Supra footnote 1.

[10] Supra footnote 3.

hand, and possibly with impatience or anger. Although not explicitly stated, the reason for this self-denial is not simply a wish to avoid wasting time and effort. Rather—and more important—subordinates wish to avoid antagonizing those whose good regard is of importance to them, perhaps because of their control of promotions and/or perhaps simply out of a desire on the part of subordinates to please their superiors. Although the point is not made explicit by Good, it is equally true that superiors seek the co-operation of subordinates upon whom they are dependent. They too must guard their words and actions in anticipation of the responses of others.

A moment's reflection reveals that, in essence, "the politics of anticipation" concept is neither more nor less than the notion that individuals behave strategically when dealing with others: most participants are playing the game to win. Moreover, the participants are not behaving, as some economic theory would assume, in splendid isolation from the needs and satisfactions of others. This holds, I think, for both superiors and subordinates. Each individual's success in satisfying his own needs is determined, in part, by his capacity to satisfy the anticipated needs of others, and vice versa. There is a kind of natural, at least partially voluntary, exchange.

The manuscript sent out for comment contained the principal conclusions that Good drew from his application of the "anticipation" concept to the budget process he was studying. This material was included with some trepidation, for the simple reason that Good's opinions could be taken to be mildly to moderately insulting. Good suggested, for example, that Finance officials faced with an opinionated Deputy held their tongues (and their pens) when they were convinced that his mind was closed to ideas at variance with his own. By implication, deputies did the same thing when dealing with opinionated ministers. Good also pressed the point that Finance officials (and presumably also ministers) formulated their budgets at least as much to avoid anticipated criticism (or gain anticipated support?) as to "do the right thing"—whatever that might be.

As it turned out, the comments received (and the refusal of one former Deputy Minister to comment at all) proved that my concern was not unwarranted. The two former deputies who did comment on the draft and one or two officials took great umbrage at Good's explanations (or is the word "charges"?). The reader will recall reactions such as "nonsense" and "how does he know?". No doubt these commentators are convinced that I showed extremely poor judgment in including Good's explanations in the manuscript.

While I regret upsetting some of the commentators—the most vociferous of whom are men of impeccable integrity—their reaction is instructive. For my part, I do not find their disavowals entirely credible. Every rational person engaged in collective decision making *must* engage in the "politics of anticipation" or, in more straightforward language, strategic behaviour (unless all the individuals involved are of like mind). The problem is that Good's "explanations," because of the way he stated them, sound like accusations of cowardice and unprincipled behaviour on the part of senior officials. The commentators' strong negative reaction is understandable.

Unfortunately, Good has had no experience, at least at the senior level, with decision-making processes in government (and, presumably, the former deputies have had no experience in writing dissertations on public administration!) If Good had had such experience, he would have realized that advisers, virtually without exception, must temper their advice to some extent in the light of their knowledge of the preferences and circumstances of the person being advised. Leaving aside those rare policy decisions that raise significant moral questions, what is the point of offering advice that is bound to be rejected and to destroy the credibility of the adviser in the eyes of the decision maker? As one experienced former Minister said, "Officials do not make a practice of offering unacceptable advice." Those who persist in so doing seldom attain the senior positions and hardly ever retain them. They might as well be dead in terms of influence. Few senior officers or ministers will spend much of their time—their most valuable resource—reading or listening to advice that they perceive to be unhelpful.

Does this mean that all successful advisers are cowardly and unprincipled? Hardly. The question cannot be answered in the abstract or in the absolute. Clearly, officials have a duty to warn their ministers of impending difficulties. They also have an obligation to suggest the alternatives available within the existing constraints (including those imposed by the ministers) and the probabilities attached to them. It is a betrayal of trust to suppress information that ministers would demand if they knew it were available. This is easily said: yet, when faced with reality, advisers have to make fine judgments concerning all these aspects of their advice, and more. Sometimes the ethical questions involved are subtle. The best advisers neither "trouble deaf heaven" nor are sycophants.

Officials who are convinced that ministers are doing or planning to do unconscionable things have a duty to resign and publicize their reasons. But senior officials cannot have their way by threatening resignation every month. (Good gives inadequate attention to this fact). In the case of a decision that is solely a matter of judgment, the judgment of the person directly responsible must prevail. Undoubtedly advisers try, and with some success, to influence the judgments of their superiors without appearing to do so. Presumably this tactic, although admittedly somewhat insidious when carried out by a master, is not perfidious if the superior has his wits about him. Sometimes it is called "education"; sometimes "brainwashing."

I believe there is nothing wrong with the concept of "the politics of anticipation," except that it is trite when understood. Good's problem is that he implies that there is some alternative. There is something silly about castigating the inevitable. What Good discovered in Finance is a universal phenomenon (except when one is making up one's own mind). Good offered no evidence to support his implicit criticism that Finance officials abused their positions by suppressing relevant information when their superiors were hostile to it. In defence of Good, it should be admitted that "the politics of anticipation" may *now* sound high-flown and suggestive of errors in judgment, if not in propriety. The concept was, however, insightful when originally presented by Wildavsky (Good's academic mentor) in his attack on rational actor models generally and especially program planning and budgeting systems. PPBS enjoyed enormous, if fleeting, favour in the 1950s and 1960s.

The Reduced Jurisdiction of the Department of Finance

It is incontestable that the jurisdiction of the Department has contracted in recent years. Three institutional changes attest to that fact:

1) the establishment in 1967 of the Treasury Board as an entity separate from Finance, with its own President and staff;

2) the establishment of the Federal-Provincial Relations Secretariat as a part of the PCO in 1975; and

3) the establishment in 1978 of the Board of Economic Development Ministers as a cabinet committee with its own ministers and staff.

In addition, there have been dramatic changes in procedures and processes. Although Finance still retains its primacy (near-monopoly?) with respect to tax structure,[11] debt management, and exchange rate mangement, even decisions in these areas involve a degree of consultation outside the Department unheard of a little more than a decade ago. Whether Finance's influence has increased with respect to policy issues other than those where it retains primacy is a moot point. One former Deputy (D2) thinks that it has. If he is correct, the explanation clearly lies in the fact that, having largely removed its pre-emptive powers, other departments and agencies, and most particularly the PCO, no longer look upon Finance as the enemy. Personally, I am skeptical that Finance has had increasing influence in those areas that are not specifically its prime responsibility. (These are noted above.) Is it credible that Finance has as much impact on federal-provincial fiscal relations and on economic and social development policies as it had when it was the overall "eco-

---

[11] This monopoly with respect to tax structure matters is now being challenged. Since the development of the tax expenditure estimates by Finance (they were tabled by John Crosbie with his budget of December 1979), cabinet committees can, at least formally, propose that certain expenditures be eliminated and the appropriate expenditure "envelope" be credited with the saving. These developments may or may not become an important feature of the tax process. It is too soon to say. Tax expenditures were explicitly introduced into the expenditure budget process in order to constrain the demand for them. The revenues forgone are to be deducted from those assigned to the policy "envelopes."

nomic manager" of the federal government? Bear firmly in mind that new agencies have been created that are now primarily responsible for these matters. To put the question slightly differently: what good is influence when the ministries of state have power? Perhaps the former Deputy was thinking of the improvement in the Department's influence in the period 1975-1979 relative to the 1968-1974 period. Had he cast his eyes back to the early 1960s, he might have been less sanguine.

Although Finance's loss of jurisdiction was dramatic, to a considerable extent the same phenomenon occurred elsewhere in the federal decision-making system. Under Mr. Trudeau, the old adversarial system, with the majority of ministers and their officials pushing single-mindedly for the interests they represented, was converted to a marked degree into a collegial system. This occurred in part because of changed circumstances and in part by design. Generally speaking, in the "old days," departments hammered out their policy proposals first within the department and then, with the blessing of their Minister, with the officials of other departments, notably Finance. By and large too, when the Minister's proposal came to Cabinet (admittedly, a proposal that took the views of other departments into account), it was a matter of acceptance or rejection, and the ultimate decision rested with the Prime Minister. Under the new approach, much of the "to-ing and fro-ing" takes place at the ministerial level in cabinet committee meetings, rather than at the stage of prior consultation with the officials of other departments. What emerges is, to a greater degree, a ministerial consensus proposal. Because proposals approved by a cabinet committee are not discussed by Cabinet as a whole, unless the issue is explicitly raised by a Minister, the impact of the Prime Minister can be slight if that is his wish. Indeed, on issues that he is not concerned about personally (such as those not related to the constitution or bilingualism!), the Prime Minister can stay aloof from the policy issue entirely, should he wish to. This seems entirely consistent with Mr. Trudeau's style and seemingly low threshold for boredom.

Two circumstances were probably important in bringing about this change. First, with increased government involvement in the economy and society, and with the federal government using a vast array of policy instruments administered by a whole panoply of departments and agencies, a decision-making system in which each department and agency stuck to its mandate had serious weaknesses. Second, Mr. Trudeau has been so pre-eminent at the polls relative to his colleagues that he is under little or no compulsion to conciliate them in order to retain their support. Few of his ministers have enough personal political leverage that they can use it to obtain the favourable decisions they want for the interests they represent. This is not to say that the interests themselves are powerless. Because of the Prime Minister's overwhelming clout, it is expedient for him to treat most of his ministers equally, but not as equals. Letting them bargain with one another is, perhaps, simply a reflection of the fact that they have no bargaining power with him.

Collegiality, *in principle,* lessens the problem of policy co-ordination. It certainly is realistic in reflecting the preponderant power of the Prime Minister. It has, however, severe drawbacks. For example, it is inordinately time consuming for ministers. It diverts their time from day-to-day departmental affairs. Ministers become more like super-bureaucrats. The resulting delays in decisions can mean the loss of strategic or tactical advantages. Probably of greater significance, collegial decisions mean collegial responsibilities. Ministers and their deputies can never be entirely sure of what is expected of them individually: matters of everyone's concern are of no one's concern. Furthermore, the interests that ministers and their departments represent are not all equal; their relative importance can and does shift with time and circumstances. Collegial decision making tends to blur these changes in the relative significance of particular conflicting interests. The resulting policies tend to be less sensitive to the often rapidly changing political and economic realities than those that would emerge from a more adversarial approach to decision making.

Secrecy

The inordinate secrecy surrounding the revenue budget process has drawn the fire of most tax practitioners and of several of our interviewees and commentators. Some, however, like former ministers M2 and M3, take a more sanguine view. The former deputies (for example, D2) are less concerned and, to a degree, defensive if not hostile to criticism of the existing provisions. One official (O1) pointed out that some of the secrecy barriers were, in fact, gradually being lowered on a highly selective basis. To support his argument, he provided some illuminating examples (cited earlier).

The secrecy problem is complicated—much more complicated than seems to be realized by those who espouse, as a tenet of small "l" liberal faith, freedom of information without qualification. Although I accept complete freedom of information as a sound starting point for those anxious to preserve (or should one say create?) a free society, reflection soon reveals the need for some limitations to full and open access. Personal privacy is, after all, a competing goal. There are at least three aspects of the secrecy issue that are highly relevant to the revenue budget process. Each is briefly discussed in turn below.

1) Personal privacy is valuable in and of itself. Probably it is also a precondition of individual liberty. Few would argue that the present high degree of confidentiality accorded personal tax information should be reduced. Indeed, as one frequently reads, further safeguards may be required to increase the protection afforded individuals against violation of their privacy by electronic means.

Maintaining confidentiality with respect to the tax records of businesses poses more controversial problems. Revealing the tax records of closely held businesses obviously can constitute a breach of personal privacy. Although not unmindful of this problem, I am not inclined to make an exception for closely held corporations above a certain size. It does not seem unreasonable to me that those who insist on secrecy should forgo the advantages of the corporate form of organization. Breaching personal privacy is not at issue, of course, for widely held businesses. And there is much to be said for giving more public access to the tax records of such corporations. For those who would not wish to proceed as far as I do, it can be argued with great force that when firms are enjoying massive amounts of tax relief via government tax concessions or direct subsidies, the public has a right to know which firms are benefiting, by how much, and the resulting changes in their profits. With this less stringent approach, those firms that were adamantly opposed to the disclosure of their tax affairs need not claim the tax relief or subsidies. If the tax records of all public firms were available for public scrutiny, disclosure would not put particular firms at a competitive disadvantage. Only if the disclosure of tax records by domestic corporations put them at a significant competitive disadvantage internationally would it be prudent to back off full disclosure of their tax accounts. Even here, given the nontraumatic experience under the American "right to know" laws, it appears unlikely that catastrophe would ensue even without specific exemptions to deal with this potential problem.

2) Insider information concerning impending or actual policy decisions sometimes provides those who obtain it with an opportunity denied to others to make profits or avoid losses. This is universally acknowledged as unfair. The possibility of making such gains is by no means confined to prior knowledge of tax policy changes. Policy changes involving expenditures, purchases, regulations, and borrowing/lending sometimes can create the same opportunities for private gain and therefore pose the same problem. Breaches of budget secrecy are no doubt made more dramatic by the extraordinary rigidity and severity of the penalties that befall a Minister of Finance who is found to have broken the secrecy rule. But, to reiterate, the difficulties in avoiding the insider information problem are common to all types of public policy decision making.

Although few of us have given the matter a moment's thought, the disclosure problem is partly a matter of mechanics. When and how and where do governments *physically* provide equal access? And to what, precisely, is access provided? Suppose that tactical considerations were not involved (an unlikely occurrence): at what stage in the development of a policy would it be reasonable to provide access? How would the government communicate to the public that the information was available? What form would that information take? Given that, in any large bureaucracy, hundreds of policy issues are being wrestled with by many people in many places on any given day, it is simply not technically feasible to provide complete access to all matters on a continuous basis. But if this kind of perfection is beyond reason, when is it reasonable and proper to provide access and how? And to what material should access be given? The basic data? All drafts? The proceedings of meetings? As a general rule, I advocate full disclosure of all basic data, with minimum restrictions (such as personal data), but no disclosure of the material developed in the often innumerable steps up to the final document. But if all earlier drafts were exempt, would there ever be a final document in most cases? Delving into the timing issue would take us too far afield.

3) Strategic and tactical considerations bulk large in most government policy decisions. Since the process is inherently adversarial (because of the fundamental fact that many of the interests being reconciled are in conflict), the government of the day, particularly under a parliamentary system, has a major strategic advantage in being able to withhold information from opponents (or, more unfortunate, in being able to provide biased or false information that opponents cannot disprove). Because oral communications are a ready, though often inconvenient and inefficient, substitute for written communications, forcing governments to disclose information that would reduce that strategic advantage simply means that those involved in decision making would do more talking (without tapes) and less writing and reading. The public would gain nothing by attempting to force such disclosure, and the process would be made more cumbersome to no purpose.

These considerations underlie the recommendations set out in the next and final section of this paper.

Budget Process Reform

Many tax practitioners are greatly exercised about the inadequacies of the process by which tax structure changes are made.[12] From what was said in Chapter 4, there seems little doubt that much of this criticism is justified. There are too many changes, and changes to changes. There are too many long periods of uncertainty that make it difficult for taxpayers to arrange their affairs in order to minimize their tax liabilities. There is too little opportunity for those representing large collective interests to bring pressure to bear on tax structure decisions. Although the tax practitioners do not complain that their incomes are growing too rapidly as a result of some of these weaknesses (and surely the weaknesses about which they complain increase the demand for their services), it is nevertheless true that a serious consequence of these impediments is the deadweight loss to society of greater and greater "transaction costs," in the parlance of economics. When all is said and done, the work of tax practitioners is unproductive labour: the time, effort, and energy involved directly or indirectly in avoiding taxes and collecting them are diverted from the production of goods and services that satisfy human needs. It should be borne in mind, too, that tax practice engages some of the ablest minds in the country. The opportunity cost to the nation is considerable.

---

[12]See, for example, Douglas Sherbaniuk, "Budget Secrecy" (May-June 1976), 24 *Canadian Tax Journal* 223-30; and Tax Legislative Process Committee, "The Tax Legislative Process" (March-April 1978), 26 *Canadian Tax Journal* 157-81.

Tax practitioners, not surprisingly perhaps, tend to take a worm's-eye view of the tax system. They would have the tax world changed to make their own lives, and those of their clients, easier. They seem to give inadequate recognition to the fact that, in a democratic society, decisions involving the resolution of conflict—that is to say, all significant tax changes—are inevitably fraught with untidiness and uncertainty. The world is already complicated and apparently is getting more complicated by the hour. Governments are intervening in more complex ways to achieve more specific, targeted ends. If one accepts this as inevitable, at least within the present context, there is nothing to be gained for society by simplifying the tax system only to shift the same kind of complexity to the expenditure or regulatory systems. Nevertheless, we can all readily agree, rather platitudinously, that any unnecessary (somehow defined) confusion, delay, and uncertainty simply add to the deadweight losses imposed by any tax system. They also bring about significant inequities.

The interviewees and commentators, on balance, supported the case for reform of the tax process. Some (such as M3), however, seemed to think it was not a serious issue or could be handled by the adoption of a more "open door" policy by Finance. One official emphasized that some improvements have already been made (for example, the Department now retains some consultants to assist in designing tax structure changes). I found the comments of a former Minister (M4) and a former Deputy Minister (D1)[13] more convincing. Both recognized the existence and significance of the problem and advanced some specific recommendations, which—although not original with them—were, coming from them, most persuasive. By merging their recommendations and adding a few minor proposals of my own, I have devised the following package for reform of the tax process.

1) A Tax Review Commission should be set up to operate along the lines of the Tariff Board, functioning as a board of inquiry. As a condition of appointment, the Commissioners should have prior detailed knowledge of taxation. The legal, accounting, and economic disciplines should be represented on the Commission and on its staff. This Commission should be required to hold hearings, issue studies, and report thereon, upon the receipt of references from the Minister of Finance or the Minister of National Revenue. *All* such studies or reports should be placed in the public domain within 30 days of their transmittal to the Minister.

The Commission should be empowered to undertake similar investigations on its own initiative or upon receipt of a request deemed by the Commission to be worthy. The terms of reference of the Commission should clearly and emphatically exclude the power to investigate any aspect of short-term fiscal policy, except in considering the transitional implications of possible structural policy changes.

---

[13] Also, to a lesser extent, D2.

In many ways, the proposed Tax Review Commission would act like a permanent Royal Commission, but at a much lower cost and, one would expect, with greater continuity. It would be important to establish the Commission as a nonpartisan body. This might be facilitated if the appointments were made in the same way as appointments to the bench and to the Office of Auditor General—after prior consultation with the respective professional groups.

2) As stated above, the Finance and Revenue Ministers should send references to the Tax Review Commission, calling for hearings, investigations, and reports. These references could take a variety of forms, from White Papers that indicate a significant degree of commitment to the principles contained in them, to more speculative colours. (If need be, a letter from the Minister spelling out the nature of a tax problem causing concern would suffice.) Copies of all references should be released upon transmittal to the Commission. Minutes could, and possibly should, specify a time within which the Commission should report back on references. (Some tax questions are perennial and without a deadline investigations could go on forever.)

3) The House Standing Committee on Finance, Trade and Economic Affairs, supported by a professional staff, should be directly involved in the budget process in two ways:

a) During the fall and winter months, the Committee should hold hearings on the "state of the economy" and its prospects, short and long run, with emphasis on the efficiency of current policies and the potential costs and benefits of alternative policies. The purpose would be to provide a forum for informed debate, in order to educate legislators and the public. It would serve as a means, ultimately, of improving the quality of government economic policies.

To minimize partisanship in the proceedings, the Committee should be empowered to prepare and circulate a synopsis of the proceedings but should *not* prepare a report that would be voted. Given the inherently partisan nature of the deliberations, the prospect of a vote would do more harm than good. To provide some incentive for MPs to participate, the materials submitted and copies of the proceedings should be disseminated as widely as possible. Televising the hearings would be desirable.

b) The Minister of Finance should table a split bill for tax measures. Changes of a nontechnical nature would be contained in that part of the bill debated in the Committee of the Whole House; changes of a technical nature (as so deemed by the Minister) would be considered by the Standing Committee. The Standing Committee should report back to the House within a specified time. The House would vote on both parts of the bill as one bill after the Committee's deliberations had been considered.

4) As an alternative to the House Committee just discussed, consideration might be given to the establishment of a Joint House-Senate Committee to

carry out the function just described. Senators have, on average, greater knowledge and experience in economic and tax matters than do members of Parliament. They also have more time available for detailed study.

5) The current general (although not invariable) practice under which tax motions become immediately effective upon tabling should be continued. As one Minister (M4) commented, because more measures are unchanged than changed as a result of subsequent debate, there is likely to be less uncertainty under the present approach than would be the case if tax bills became effective only upon Royal Proclamation.

6) It is not recommended that the Minister issue what would be, in effect, a draft revenue budget for consideration by the parliamentary committee. The prior public discussion of possible technical changes could better take place before the proposed Tax Review Commission on a reference from the Minister. A "pre-budget" document would invariably generate a highly partisan debate in the Committee. I also take seriously the point made by a former Minister (M3) that, to the extent that a budget is an exercise in persuasion, the Minister of Finance needs the drama of budget night.

7) The gross imbalance between the pressure exerted on public decision makers by narrow interest groups, on the one hand, and those representing more general interests, on the other, is well known. Small groups with much at stake for each member find it infinitely easier to organize and finance their lobbying and public relations activities than do large groups with an ill-defined interest. The latter are likely to be relatively weak where the amounts at stake in aggregate are large but, on a per-member basis, are small. These "public-interest" groups, when they do form, are bedevilled by the "free-rider" problem: the individuals who collectively constitute "the public" wish the organization to succeed in order that they may obtain the benefits of the successful exercise of pressure. But the same individuals hope even more that someone else will bear the costs of the organization. The problem is as ubiquitous as it is difficult to resolve.

To a limited extent, the Canadian Tax Foundation serves the counterbalancing "collective interest representation" function. By its research, conferences, and publications, which include the views of informed academics, it exerts some effort to disseminate "public interest" tax analyses and proposals. One can hardly, however, expect the members of the Foundation to take on the full burden of what, in essence, is a charitable exercise. One hesitates, too, to suggest that the government subsidize the Foundation in order that it may give greater emphasis to its public interest role. Such a move might be seen to detract from the objectivity, impartiality, and political neutrality that characterize its activities. I am likewise reluctant to recommend government support for some kind of tax research/public education institute for the purpose of improving the balance of pressure on public decision makers. There are enough research centres and institutes now on the scene, although admittedly none devotes its efforts exclusively to tax analyses, and some face perpetual financing problems.

Although not totally satisfactory, the first step I recommend is that provision be made in the budgets of the proposed Tax Review Commission and of the Standing Committee for funds to commission studies and finance the appearance of witnesses. Independent specialists would be paid, in effect, to reveal the "other side of the story," insofar as special interests are concerned.[14] These commissioned studies and retained expert witnesses would preclude the necessity of a large permanent research staff for either the proposed Tax Review Commission or for the parliamentary committee.

---

[14]This idea has been discussed by Michael Trebilcock, J. Robert S. Pritchard, and L. Waverman, "The Consumer Interest and the Regulatory Process," in A. J. Duggan and L. J. Darvall, eds., *Consumer Protection Law and Theory* (Agincourt, Ont.: Carswell, 1980), 256-69; and Michael Trebilcock and Ken Engelhart, *Public Participation in Collective Decision-making* (Ottawa: Economic Council of Canada, forthcoming).

Index

Accountability, 42-45
  and budget secrecy, 41, 55
  of Department of Finance, 42,
    43

Bank of Canada
  relationship with Department of
    Finance, 8-10
  responsibility for monetary
    policy, 8-10
Board of Economic Development
  Ministers, 12, 39
Breton, Albert
  and economic advisers to Prime
    Minister, 38
Budget
  complexity, 35, 47
  presentation, changes
    recommended, 55-57
  process, suggestions for reform,
    48-49, 70-74
  secrecy, 25-26, 32, 38, 39-41,
    49, 68
    abandonment recommended,
      5
  reasons for, 2, 68-69
  speech, 26-27
  timing, 25
    passage through Parliament,
      35
Business Council on National Issues
  suggested Joint House of Com-
    mons-Senate Committee, 52

Cabinet
  committee system, 4, 33, 39, 66,
    67
  government, 2-3
  influence on budget, 30, 38,
    42-43
Cabinet Committee on Economic
  Development, 12, 39
Canadian Tax Foundation, 73

on amendments to budgets, 34
report on budget secrecy, 49
suggestion for parliamentary
  committee, 51
on use of outside advisers, 57
Carter Commission See Royal Commission on Taxation
Collegial government, 38, 67-68
Committee of Ministers of Finance
  and Provincial Treasurers, 11
Continuing Committee on Fiscal
  and Economic Matters, function,
  10-11
Cook, Gail
  parliamentary committee recom-
    mended, 52

Decision-making
  basis, 6-23
  process, 24-31, 38, 42-45, 61-66
  quality, 21-22, 34, 45
Department of Finance
  accountability, 42-45
  Budget Committee, 26-27
  decision-making See Decision-
    making
  information sources, 7-21, 41,
    74
  membership of interdepart-
    mental committees, 13
  relationship with
    Bank of Canada, 8-10, 36
    Minister of Finance, 36-37,
      42
    other federal departments,
      12-16, 66-67
    provincial governments, 10-
      12, 40
    the public, 16-20, 40, 71-74
  role in government, 3-4, 66-68
Departmental jurisdictions, 12-16,
  32, 37-39, 66-67

Econometric models, use in forecasting, 20-21
Economic advisers, 38, 39
Economic analysis, 17, 19, 20-22,
26
Economic policy
committees to examine, 50-52
government accountability, 55
Envelope system, 54
defined, 4
Expenditure envelopes *See* Envelope
system
Explanatory material, with budget
papers, 47, 57

Fiscal policy, 6, 8-10, 36
discussion before budget, 51
measures separate in budget bills,
recommended, 57
Five-year fiscal plans, 52-55

Interdepartmental committees, 13

Joint House of Commons-Senate
committee, recommended, 52,
72-73
Jurisdictional disputes *See* Departmental jurisdictions

Lambert Commission *See* Royal
Commission on Financial Management and Accountability

Minister of Finance
relationship with
Department of Finance, 36-
37
Prime Minister, 3, 25, 27-29,
42
responsibilities in cabinet, 3
Monetary policy, 36
Bank of Canada's responsibilities,
8-10

Outside advisers, use, 17-18, 38, 49,
57

Parliament, input on budget, 43, 56
Parliamentary committees, 5, 47,
51-60, 72-74
Prime Minister
influence on budget, 28-29, 42
relationship with Minister of
Finance, 3, 25, 27-29

Privacy, personal, 68

Revenue budget, nature, 6
Royal Commission on Financial
Management and Accountability
fiscal plan recommended, 53-55,
59-60
parliamentary committees, 5
Royal Commission on Taxation
budget secrecy, 48
suggested Tax Advisory Committee, 49

Sherbaniuk, D. J.
parliamentary committee to
study tax changes, 51
proposed Tax Review Board, 50
Standing Committee on Finance,
Trade and Economic Affairs
preliminary examination of
budget proposals, 56, 57, 72
taxation subcommittee recommended, 51

Tax advisory committees, proposed,
47, 49-51
Tax expenditures, 4, 14-15
defined, 35
Tax legislation, examination, 49-50
Tax policy, 18, 22, 26, 57-58
measures separate in budget bills,
recommended, 57-58
Tax records, confidentiality, 68-69
Tax Reform Bill, 1971, procedure
outlined, 55-56
Tax Review Board, proposed, 50
Tax Review Commission, proposed,
71-72, 74
Tax structure
amendments to recent budgets,
34
changes sent to parliamentary
committees, recommendation,
58
process for change, 70-74
Timing
adoption of tax measures, 35,
73
budget, 22, 25-28
budget speech, 28

White papers, use recommended,
47, 55-56